11 Plus C.E.M. Style Verbal Ability Workbook
© P.R. and C.R. Draper 2018

The answers are available separately or at:
http://www.achieve2day.co.uk/workbooks

All rights reserved. No part of this book may be reproduced or transmitted in any form or by any means without written permission of the author.

Published: achieve2day, Slough, 2015
ISBN: 978-1-909986-11-4

Contents

Chapter 1: Nouns and articles

1.1 Nouns

There are different parts of speech.

On	Wednesday	Amy	went	to	the	local
•preposition	•proper noun	•proper noun	•verb	•preposition	•article	•adjective

cinema	while	we	quickly	shopped	.
•common noun	•connective	•pronoun	•adverb	•verb	•punctuation

A noun is a naming word. Nouns name things, places and ideas.

Nouns are either common nouns or proper nouns. Common nouns are used to describe everyday objects, places, people and ideas. The word "the" can be placed immediately before a common noun and it will make sense.
Proper nouns are the names given to specific people, places, animals or ideas. Proper nouns always start with a capital letter. Some words become a proper noun when the word "the" is placed in front. So, a queen is a female ruler but The Queen in England refers to Queen Elizabeth II.

Types of common noun

Type of common noun	Description	Examples
Concrete	Can be seen and touched	book, planet
Abstract	Cannot be touched	beauty, love
Collective	A group of things, animals or people	stack, flock, crowd

Types of proper noun

Type of proper noun	Example
People	Beth, Ian Milne, the Duchess of Canterbury
Titles	Mr, Mrs, Dr, Sir, Professor, Reverend
Time	Wednesday, September
Places	England, London, North Sea, Europe
Buildings	Eiffel Tower
Institutions	Oxford University, Great Ormond Street Hospital for Children.
Historical events and periods	The Medieval ages, Roman Empire, World War I
Events and festivals	Olympic Games, Christmas Day
Religious names	Christianity, Judaism, Muslim, Bible

One way of identifying a noun is to put the word "the" in front of it and if the resulting combination makes sense, the word is a noun. However, this does not work for some proper nouns. For example we never put the word "the" in front of England or Europe. Be careful, adjectives can be put between "the" and the noun, but while "the young calf" makes sense, "the young" doesn't, so young is not a noun.

Exercise 1.1
Underline the word which is a noun
1. catty, quickly, shoe, hard
2. slope, timely, blue, fasten
3. honest, truthfully, glad, honesty
4. bake, shape, abide, imagine

Choose which word is a proper noun
5. City, London, Country, Train
6. Wednesday, Month, Time, Season
7. Book, Film, Nile, Pharaoh

Choose which word can be used as a proper noun
8. song, headteacher, secretary, beauty
9. relative, family, father, friend

10. What type of noun is the word "truth"? _____

1.2 Pronouns

A pronoun is a word that takes the place of a noun.

There are many different types of pronoun including:
Personal pronouns
Subjective
Objective
Possessive
Reflexive
Impersonal pronouns
Indefinite

The subjective pronouns are I, you, he, she, it, we and they.
Subjective pronouns act as the subject of the sentence. That is the person or thing that has been replaced by the pronoun does the action in the sentence.
eg. **He** kicked the ball.

The objective pronouns are me, you, him, her, it and them.
Objective pronouns act as the object of the sentence. That is the verb is being done to the person or thing that the pronoun has replaced.
eg. The boy kicked **it**.

The table below summarises the use of subjective and objective pronouns.

	Subjective		Objective	
	Singular	Plural	Singular	Plural
1st person	I	we	me	us
2nd person	you	you	you	you
3rd person	he / she / it	they	him / her / it	them

The possessive pronouns are: mine, yours, hers, his, ours and theirs.
Possessive pronouns refer to something owned or belonging to the author or someone mentioned in the sentence previously.
eg. It is **his** ball.

The reflexive pronouns are: myself, yourself, himself, herself, itself, ourselves, yourselves and themselves.
Reflexive pronouns refer back to the subject or clause.
eg. He hurt **himself**.

Indefinite pronouns, also called impersonal pronouns include: somebody, someone, something, anybody, anyone, anything, nobody, no one, nothing, everybody, everyone and everything.
Indefinite pronouns are used when it is not a specific person, thing or group being referred to.
Eg. **Everybody** enjoyed the concert.   or   **Nobody** came.

Exercise 1.2
Write the correct pronoun to replace the underlined word(s).

1. **Richard** was very hungry.   _____

2. Simran really loved **the flowers**.   _____

3. This is **my family's** car.   _____

4. He kicked **the rock** and broke his toe.   _____

5. Suddenly the bird flew towards **Alice**.   _____

Fill in the blanks with the appropriate pronoun.

6. Steven really loved _____ new baby sister.

7. Luke tied his shoelaces _____.

8. My friend and _____ are going to the cinema.

9. The five mile walk follows the river. _____ takes you past the ruins of an old castle.

10. My aunt read a story to Sufyan and _____.

1.3 The Articles
The indefinite article is 'a' or 'an.'
The definite article is 'the.'

The indefinite article, 'a' or 'an', is used to refer to something that is not specific or something that we have not mentioned before. e.g. I had a sandwich for lunch. 'A' is used if the next word starts with a consonant and 'an' is used when the next word starts with a vowel. Sometimes we use 'an' before the letter 'h.' For example: I was running an hour late.

The definite article is used to refer to a specific person or thing. So 'a tree' refers to any tree while 'the tree' refers to a particular tree.

There are three main rules in using articles.
1. When we say people's jobs or careers we use the indefinite article.
   eg. She is a doctor or He is an architect.
2. Singular countable nouns always have an article (a, an or the) or another determiner such as my, your, this or that.
   eg. I saw **a** play at **the** theatre.
3. When we write about things in general we use no article.
   eg. Children start secondary school at age 11.
   Children has no article because its referring to children in general.
   However, we could write "The children start school on Monday" if we are talking about a particular group of children.

Exercise 1.3

In each of the sentences below decide whether the space should be: 'a', 'an', 'the' or nothing. Put a 'dash' if the space should be left blank.

1. The class behaved so badly _____ teacher was in tears.

2. She was really hoping for _____ puppy for Christmas.

3. _____ hill was very steep and we were exhausted when we reached the top.

4. We were amazed by _____ beauty at the top of the hill.

5. There are _____ couple of possibilities.

6. The fourth planet from the Sun is _____ Mars.

7. My appointment was _____ Wednesday before last.

8. Whatever, _____ weather, the move will go ahead as planned.

9. Many dinosaurs became extinct at the end of _____ Cretaceous period.

10. There was _____ accident on the motorway.

Chapter 2: Verbs

2.1 Verbs

A verb is a word that describes what a person, animal or thing is doing or being.

There are two types of verbs:

      Action verbs, eg. jump, run, sing, think

      Being verbs (also called linking verbs), eg. to be, become and have.

Verbs can be written in the past, present or future tense.

In regular verbs the present tense are all the same except the he / she / it (3rd person singular) when an 's' is added.

For example: the verb to walk.

I	walk
You	walk
He / she / it	walks
We	walk
You	walk
They	walk

Exercise 2.1

Complete each sentence with the correct present tense of the verb in brackets.

1. Tony _____ to his favourite music. (listen)
2. Craig _____ the cricket ball over the fence. (hit)
3. I _____ playing computer games but Mum _____ them. (like / hate)
4. Rithvik _____ that he is OK. (say)
5. Dad _____ to work very early. (go)
6. He _____ his laptop everywhere. (carry)
7. Dr Overton _____ her patient. (examine)

Underline the linking verbs in the sentences below.

8. "You have become very tall," exclaimed his aunt.
9. He is very naughty and was caught throwing cushions.
10. The kitchen floor seems dirty, so I will wash it after dinner.

2.2 Irregular verbs.

Not all verbs are regular. Two irregular verbs that you need to know are "to be" and "to have."

to be		to have	
I	am	I	have
you	are	you	have
he/she/it	is	he/shje/it	has
we	are	we	have
they	are	they	have

Exercise 2.2
Complete each sentence, in the present tense, using verb 'to be' or 'to have'.

1. I _____ very hungry.

2. It _____ very cold in London today.

3. We _____ very happy that the holidays start next week.

4. She _____ a beautiful smile.

5. We _____ almost ready.

6. They _____ very angry.

7. _____ it finished yet?

8. He _____ a love of cooking.

9. They _____ practicing for the concert.

10. It _____ a secret.

2.3 Past tense

To make a verb into the past tense we add 'ed.'
eg., I walked.

If the verb finishes with a 'y', then we change the 'y' to an 'i' and add 'ed'.
eg. cry becomes cried.

If the verb ends with an 'e', then we remove the 'e' before adding 'ed'.
eg. smile becomes smiled.

Many verbs are irregular. Such as:

find →found

drive → drove

eat → ate

see → saw

grow → grew

Another form of the past tense is the past Perfect, which shows that something occurred before another action or a specific time in the past. This form of the past tense uses the word 'has', 'have' or 'was.' So the past tense of 'show' is 'showed', but the past perfect is 'have shown'.

Exercise 2.3
Write the simple past tense (one word) for the following verbs

    1. Find   _____

    2. Fly   _____

    3. Speak   _____

    4. Light   _____

    5. Blow   _____

    6. Slide   _____

Complete each sentence with the past tense of the verb in brackets.

7. I _____ to Spain last holiday. (to go)

8. It _____ snowing a lot last week. (to be)

9. Mark _____ in the park, for an hour. (play)

10. He _____ the ball. (catch)

2.4 Future Tense and Present continuous tense.

To put verbs into the future tense, you can either:
    Add 'will' before the verb, or
    eg. I will walk.
    Add the verb 'to be' followed by 'going to'.
    eg. I am going to walk.

The future tense never appears in sentences that begin with a word that refers to time such as when, while, before, after, by the time, as soon as, unless etc.
So it should be: When you arrive. NOT When you will arrive.

For a continuous action we use the verb 'to be' followed be the verb with 'ing' added.
    eg. I am walking.

Complete the following sentences, in the future tense. Put a 'dash' if the space should be left blank.

1. Tomorrow, I _____ go and see the doctor.

2. Unless, you _____ hand it in tomorrow, you will get a detention.

3. She is _____ to see what she can do.

4. Next week we _____ on holiday.

5. I notice the photocopier has stopped _____, so I will call a repairman to come look at it. (work)

6. He _____ hoping, for some more clients.

7. When you _____ come and visit, I will show you around.

8. It is going to _____ a hot summer.

9. I am very tired so I am _____ to bed.

10. It is very late, when _____ you stop working?

Chapter 3: Adjectives and adverbs

3.1 Adjectives

An adjective describes a noun.

Many nouns can be changed into adjectives by adding 'y', 'ful', 'able', 'ing' or 'less' as a suffix.
e.g. bear + able becomes bearable.

Exercise 3.1
Complete the following sentences by using the adjective derived from the word in brackets.

1. She always completed the work on time. She was very _____. (rely)

2. He was always a very polite, efficient and _____ young man. (respect)

3. She had a pair of _____, new shoes. (shine)

4. She was very _____ and offered to do Jenny's shopping while Jenny's arm was broken. (thought)

5. He was very _____ to receive the lovely retirement gift. (thank)

6. She was very _____, that she was not allowed to go to the zoo when her friends were going. (resent)

7. He had a very _____ trip to the museum. (enjoy)

8. She didn't think of others because she was always so _____. (self)

9. He found the toolbox very _____. (use)

10. It was cold and _____ with rain. (pour)

3.2 Comparatives and superlatives

Besides giving extra detail about a noun, adjectives can also be used to compare things. Comparatives are used to compare two things, or to say that one thing is more or less than the other. Superlatives are used to state which one is the most of something. Comparatives are normally formed by adding the suffix 'er,' while superlatives are formed by adding the suffix 'est.'

However, there are many exceptions. For example you may have heard the poem.

Good, better best, never let it rest,
Until the good is better and the better is best.

Similarly, the comparative of bad is worse and the superlative is worst.

Exercise 3.2
Complete the following sentences by adding the correct suffix to the word in brackets.

1. It was cold here today but in Scotland it was even _____. (cold)

2. Mum stopping me using the computer is the _____ punishment. (bad)

3. It was the _____ thing she had ever done. (hard)

4. The movie was even _____ than the book. (scary)

5. The hare ran _____ than the tortoise. (fast)

6. This computer is certainly _____ but it is more expensive. (good)

7. He was the _____ in his class. (tall)

8. The balloon got _____ and _____ and now it is the _____. (big)

9. Her hair becomes much _____ in humid conditions. (curly)

10. She was a very lazy student and did the _____ amount of work possible. (less)

3.3 Adverbs

Adverbs are words that describe a verb, an adjective or another adverb. Most adverbs end with the suffix 'ly.'
eg. quick becomes quickly.
However, there are a large number of irregular adverbs such as just and late.

Exercise 3.3
Complete the following sentences by adding a suitable adverb. Do so by adding the correct suffix to the word in brackets when appropriate.

1. He _____ jumped over the fence. (quick)

2. He handed in his assignment _____ in time.

3. He can _____ run 100m in twelve seconds. (usual)

4. Cut _____ around the dotted lines. (careful)

5. I _____ ran out of time. (consequence)

6. The cat stretched _____ in the sun. (lazy)

7. He _____ helped him Mum to cook dinner. (happy)

8. The factory is _____ accessible by road. (easy)

In the sentences below, underline the best adverb.

9. We have to leave (soon, sometime, never, just)

10. He has (soon, going, almost, clear) finished his essay.

Chapter 4: Small words

4.1 Connectives

Connectives join two parts of a sentence. They can also be called conjunctions.

Connectives can have a number of different effects as shown in the table below.

Effect	Example
Cause and effect	Since, consequently, therefore, because
Sequence, time	Since, then, next, before, when, while
Comparison	However, although, whereas, nevertheless, compared with
Emphasis	Particularly, especially, clearly, above all
Illustration	For example, as shown by
Addition	Also, and, too, again, as well as, furthermore

Exercise 4.1
Underline the best connective in the sentences below.

1. I waited at home (when, until, because, since) the ambulance arrived.
2. I understand that we are not going ahead (since, therefore, however, when) can you tell me the reasons?
3. She jumped (although, because, finally, and) she saw a very large spider.
4. The game ended (until, furthermore, again, when) the referee blew his whistle.
5. He couldn't spell that word (so, although, if, next) he looked it up in the dictionary.
6. We arrived home on time (because, since, although, consequently) the flight was delayed by half an hour.
7. We called a plumber (because, since, although, consequently) the boiler broke down in our home.
8. We had lunch, (although, because, then, again) went to the park.
9. Suzy and I went shopping (since, after, because, however) watching a movie at the cinema.
10. Arun couldn't go to school (until, because, although, however) it was snowing.

4.2 Prepositions

A word that is used in front of a noun or pronoun to show place, time, direction or method.

eg. We went **by** train.

Common prepositions include: down, through, of, for, by, in, over, under, before, after, from, in front, behind, beside and to.

Exercise 4.2

Underline the words below that are prepositions

1. jump, over, in, under, quickly, fast

2. when, before, of, through, as, against

3. after, hill, next to, by, about, during, daughter

4. object, someone, into, within, tomorrow, outside

Underline the preposition in the sentences below.

5. They raced down the hill.

6. The sign was leaning against the tree.

7. He was afraid of the dark.

Complete the sentences below by writing 'in' or 'on.'

8. All the family came to lunch_____ Christmas Day.

9. They are going to Wales _____ June.

10. What are you doing _____ the weekend?

Chapter 5: Beginning and ending sentences

5.1 Capital letters

Capital letters are used for the following:
- Beginning of sentences.
  eg. **E**very sentence begins with a capital letter.
- Proper nouns.
  eg. On **T**uesday, **J**ohn went for a swim.
- Beginning of speech.
  eg. Jeevan muttered, "**O**ne day, I will do it even better."
- Some units or pieces of equipment are capitalised if they are named after a person.
  eg. Force is measured in **N**ewtons.
- Some abbreviations use capital letters.
  eg. The documentary on the BBC was excellent.

Exercise 5.1
Circle the letters in the sentences below that should be capital.

1. are you free next wednesday?

2. the temperature was minus two degrees celcius.

3. "please come to my party," said robert.

4. he asked the teacher how to calculate a mean, "like this," the teacher replied.

5. she bought 3 kilograms of meat from the fine cuts butchers.

6. the hospital warned that car parking was limited on south street.

7. an adverb is a word that describes a verb.

8. the duke and duchess of cambridge's first child is prince william.

9. finally, mr smith said that his daughter could go to the party in london.

10. he was able to speak french and swahili fluently, which was very helpful when visiting east africa.

5.2 Ending Sentences

All sentences must end with some punctuation.

Most sentences end with a full-stop. Full stops are also used to show that a word has been abbreviated. For example: Dr. stands for doctor; Aug. stands for August; Jr. stands for junior. Most acronyms are written without full-stops. For example: NASA or DNA. If an abbreviation comes at the end of a sentence only one full-stop is used.

Questions end with a question mark (?). For example: "Why?" or "You don't think I could do a good job, do you?"

Exclamation marks (!) can be used to end orders or for emphasis. Exclamation marks often express surprise or astonishment. For example: Stop! or That's so scary!

Ellipses (...) are used to show that text has been omitted in a quotation or it indicates that a sentence has been left unfinished. For example: "On Saturday at the School Fair there will be lots of stalls ... students are not expected to come in school uniform." or "It was a long time ago, as I remember it now, when ..."

Exercise 5.2
End each sentence with the correct punctuation.

1. It is still three weeks before half term
2. Can you come here now, please
3. When will the books be ready
4. Come, now
5. I was wondering
6. It is so exciting
7. Christmas Day is celebrated on the 25th of December
8. The party starts at 4:00 p.m
9. The teacher asked me if I understood long division
10. Help

Chapter 6: Commas

6.1 Phrases and Clauses

A phrase is a group of words that does not contain a verb. A clause does contain a verb.
For example: The sun is round, like a ball.
"The sun is round" is a clause because it contains a verb, while "like a ball" does not contain a verb so it a phrase.

A clause that makes sense on its own is the main clause, while a clause that does not is called a sub-ordinate clause.

Exercise 6.1
State if the following are clauses (C) or phrases (P).

1. The orange butterfly   _____

2. Already making cards   _____

3. The friendly giant lived in a humble cottage   `_____

4. The difficult test   _____

State whether the underlined part of the sentences below are phrases (P), sub-ordinate clauses (SO) or the main clause (MC).

5. <u>The students filed out of the classroom silently</u>, when the fire-alarm rang.

                                                                                      _____

6. She danced <u>every Saturday morning.</u>   _____

7. <u>While she was singing</u>, the audience were mesmerised.   _____

8. The dance was held <u>in the community centre hall.</u>   _____

9. <u>There was an accident on the motorway</u>, resulting in severe delays during peak hour.   _____

10. <u>Even though it was cold outside</u>, she felt hot.   _____

6.2 Clauses and commas

Commas are used to separate the main clause from the rest of the sentence. However, commas are not needed immediately before a connective.

So, if you can remove part of a sentence and the sentence still make sense, commas should be put around that additional information.

For example: On Saturday after the movies we went out for lunch.
If I remove the phrase "after the movies" the sentence "On Saturday we went out for lunch" still makes sense. So I put commas around this phrase and the sentence reads: On Saturday, after the movies, we went out for lunch.

Exercise 6.2
Put commas in the following sentences:

1. Ruth loved all food particularly pasta.

2. C.S. Lewis who is mostly known for the Narnia Chronicles wrote many books.

3. Anthony wanted to play with his friends though he really needed to finish his homework.

4. The biology course which is very intensive is finishing on Friday.

5. Since they installed the new run the hens have been laying lots of eggs.

6. You must wash your hands even if they look clean after taking the rubbish out.

7. He loved reading all books though historical adventure books were his favourite.

8. Although many considered themselves knowledgeable the results revealed a lack of knowledge.

9. By the time we got home the movie we really wanted to watch had finished.

10. In a food chain not all the energy taken in by an organism passes to the next organism.

6.3 Commas and lists

Commas are used to separate simple items in a list.
For example: Make sure you bring a torch, notebook, pen and towel to camp.

Lists of adjectives are separated by commas.
For example: The beautiful, large, blue butterfly fluttered away.

Whether, a comma is placed before the word "and" is optional. The comma before the "and" is known as the serial comma or the Oxford comma. However, it is necessary when it is needed for the sentence to be unambiguous.
For example: The meal contained soup, salad, and macaroni and cheese.

Exercise 6.3

Put commas in the following sentences:

1. Please buy some cheese ham apples bananas and bread on your way home.

2. Please can I have the large red book?

3. The colours of the spectrum are: red orange yellow green blue indigo and violet.

4. For homework you must complete: the definitions crossword and practice questions.

5. Anyone who wishes to succeed as a scientist must have: dedication excellent time management skills good knowledge and an ability to think logically.

6. Finally Mark Matthew Jason Ansha and Diya arrived.

7. I tried her home mobile and work numbers, but could not contact her.

8. Choices of meal included: spaghetti fried rice stir fry and sausages and eggs.

9. Go past the old church turn left at the end of the road turn right at the park and my house is third on the left

10. She did lots of afterschool activities including: netball science club computing and film club.

6.4 Other uses of Commas

Other uses of commas include:
- Separating a quotation, such as speech, from the rest of the sentence.
  For example: She thought and then replied, "I really should have studied more."
- To separate an introductory word from the rest of the sentence.
  For example: Sorry, I am already busy. However, I can come on Sunday.
- Surrounding the word, however, in a sentence.
  For example: Hundreds of people flocked into the city, however, the crowds dispersed quickly.
- To separate the name of a city or town from the county or country.
  For example: We went to Barcelona, Spain.
- To separate elements of time, such as days, months and years.
  For example: The school term finishes on Friday, 17th July.

Finally, commas are used whenever they are needed to avoid ambiguity (ambiguity means it can have more than one possible meaning).
For example: She fed her cat, food.   or   She fed her, cat food.

Exercise 6.4
Put commas into the following sentences:

1. "Please can I go to the party" he begged.

2. She lives in Burnham Buckinghamshire.

3. "Hi how are you?"

4. However I am in good health.

5. Wait I will think about it.

6. Yes I would like a cup of tea please.

7. "They have forecast rain" he reported.

8. The cyclone hit Darwin Australia.

9. We moved in December 2011.

10. Unfortunately we do not have enough time.

Chapter 7: Colons and Semi-colons

7.1 Colons

There are three main uses of a colon:
- To introduce a list. However, do not use a colon to introduce a list if the word immediately preceding the first item is a verb or preposition.
  For example: Please remember to bring the following: pen, ruler, rubber and calculator.
- Between two clauses when the second clause explains or follows from the first.
  For example: I'll tell you what I'm going to do: I'm going to quit!
- Before a quotation or direct speech.
  For example: The headline read: "Homework Improves Student Grades."

Exercise 7.1
Put a colon and commas if needed into the following sentences.

1. The potion contained frogs' legs snails and unicorn horns.

2. There was only one way he could pass he had to practice every day.

3. I have invited the following people to my party Amy Simona and Andrea.

4. You only have one choice leave while you can.

5. You must bring to the exam two pencils a rubber a pencil sharpener a bottle of water and a small snack.

6. You must persevere and try hard. Remember the quotation "Aim for the moon. If you miss, you may hit a star."

7. Hurry I can't wait long.

8. Remember what our teacher always said "Always treat others with respect."

9. There are many gaming platforms such as the Wii Nintendo DS X-box the PlayStation and the PC.

10. Punctuation it makes language easier to understand.

7.2 Semi-colons to join sentences

Semi-colons can be used to join two independent clauses, where the clauses can each stand separately and are closely related.
For example: In class you are to complete the crossword and exam-style questions; what you do not finish is homework.

A semi-colon can always be replaced with either a full-stop or a comma and the word "and".
So the above sentence could read:
- In class you are to complete the crossword and exam-style questions. What you do not finish is homework.

                    or
- In class you are to complete the crossword and exam-style questions, and what you do not finish is homework.

Exercise 7.2
Can these sentences be joined with a semi-colon?

1. The young boy loved playing with Lego. It is soon his birthday.   _____

2. He was a great writer. Recently he won a writing competition.   _____

3. Many people like burgers. He rowed his boat into the stream.   _____

4. The fair was very loud. It went on very late.   _____

5. My teacher is going bald. His hairline is receding quickly.   _____

Are the semi-colons in these sentences correct?

6. My new boss has many great traits; kind, friendly and fair.   _____

7. My mother wants the table cleared; or she gets very grumpy.   _____

8. Her new book is well written; it has already sold many copies.   _____

9. No one was seriously hurt in the accident; one man suffered a broken arm.   _____

10. The meal was a great success; despite the late change in plans.   _____

7.3 Semi-colons in lists

Semi-colons are used instead of commas in complex lists, particularly lists that already contain commas.

For example: On holidays we went to: Paris, France; Vienna, Austria; Rome, Italy; Madrid, Spain and Brussels, Belgium.

A study of 16 to 23 year olds in Britain showed that: 40% of those surveyed did not know that milk comes from a cow; nearly 33% did not know that eggs come from hens; 7% thought that eggs come from wheat and 36% did not know that bacon comes from pigs.

Exercise 7.3
Circle the commas which should be semi-colons.
1. For lunch you can choose: ham, cheese or chicken sandwiches, tea, coffee or hot chocolate, and apple pie, chocolate brownie or ice-cream sundae.

2. For her school project, she had to write a biography. She could choose from: Wolfgang Amadeus Mozart, the composer, Florence Nightingale, the nurse, Christopher Columbus, the explorer or Edward Jenner, the doctor.

3. In the meeting today we have Richard Smith, Curtin University, Andrew McGowan, Yale, Alister McGrath, Oxford University and Patrick Flynn, Cambridge University.

4. Cows are very useful as they give us: milk, which contains lots of nutrients, meat is high in protein and leather which makes the best shoes.

5. For Christmas I sent cards to many places, such as: Dodoma, Tanzania, Tansen, Nepal and Perth, Australia.

The following lists are unpunctuated. You need to decide if a colon is needed to introduce the list and to decide on the correct punctuation to separate the elements in the list.

6. She had lots of homework including an essay for English a lab report for Science a past paper for Maths and another essay for History.

7. Here are the directions leave the M4 at Junction 7 turn left at the round-about and then left at Langley High Street.

8. When trying to work out who to dress up as for book-week, he considered Harry Potter Charlie Bucket Charlie and the Chocolate Factory Peter The Narnia Chronicles or Aslan also from the Narnia Chronicles.

9. Some places I still want to visit in Europe are Prague Czech Republic Berlin Germany Copenhagen Denmark Vienna Austria and the Greek Islands.

10. For parents evening, my parents needed to see Dr Simpson Science Mr Maughan English Miss Cleghorne History Mr Groves Maths Mme Moreau French and Mr Money Business Studies.

Chapter 8: Apostrophes

8.1 Belonging

Apostrophes are used to show possession. The apostrophe is placed after the person (or thing) that owns the other noun. If the person or thing does not end in an 's', an 's' is placed after the apostrophe.

For example: The boy's books. Means the books belonging to a boy.
       The boys' books. Means the books belonging to two or more boys.

The exception is its.

Exercise 8.1
Re-write the following using an apostrophe.

1. The pen belonging to my Dad.   _____

2. The lead for the dog.   _____

3. The collar of the shirt.   _____

4. The dresses of the bridesmaids.   _____

5. The car belonging to the family.   _____

6. The wife of his boss.   _____

7. The computer belonging to James.   _____

8. The party for the children.   _____

9. The edge of the box.   _____

10. The lyrics of the songs.   _____

8.2 Contractions

Apostrophes can also be used to form a contraction. In a contraction the apostrophe stands in the place of the missing letters.

For example: "can not" can be shortened to "can't"; the apostrophe standing for the space, 'n' and 'o'.

Two exceptions are "will not" and "shall not." The contractions are won't and shan't.

Exercise 8.2
Write the contractions for the following phrases.

1. is not   _____

2. we are   _____

3. who will   _____

4. I have   _____

5. I am   _____

6. could have   _____

7. they are   _____

8. where did   _____

9. let us   _____

10. they would   _____

8.3 Its

So that there is a difference between "its" meaning possession and "its" as a contraction, "its" is a special case.

- It's with an apostrophe means it is or it has.
- Its without an apostrophe means something belonging to it.

It is easy to remember which one is which. Just remember "It's an apostrophe."

If you can replace the word "its" with "it is" or "it has", then it should have an apostrophe. If neither makes sense then it should be "its", without the apostrophe.

Exercise 8.3
Complete the sentences below with its or it's.

1. _____ time for dinner.

2. My hair is losing _____ colour.

3. I don't think _____ going to be finished on time.

4. The dog buried _____ bone.

5. _____ getting cold outside.

6. _____ hoof was injured, so the horse was unable to compete.

7. Our school is very proud of _____ students.

8. The dragon was tame but _____ breath was horrid.

9. I don't get on with the printer, _____ got another paper jam.

10. I've put the kettle on, please let me know when _____ boiling.

Chapter 9: Other Punctuation

9.1 Speech marks or Quotation marks

Quotation marks are always used in pairs with " to introduce the quote and " to end it.

Quotation marks are used for the following:

- To surround direct speech.
- To surround a quote.
- To separate particular words or phrases.
- To surround the title of a book, film or article.

Single inverted commas are used to surround quotes within quotes.

When writing speech, remember:

- The first word of speech in the sentence should start with a capital letter.
- Speech should be surrounded by commas, where there is no other punctuation.

Exercise 9.1
Punctuate the following:

1. Are we there yet they chorused.

2. What do you want to drink he was asked.

3. He really enjoyed reading The Magician's Nephew by C.S. Lewis.

4. I don't believe you she said you never tell the truth.

5. As Nelson Mandela once said Education is the most powerful weapon which you can use to change the world.

6. Excuse me I said do you have the time?

7. Anna suggested that Frozen would be a fun movie to watch.

8. She read so many of the Secret Seven by Enid Blyton she considered the characters her friends.

9. Mum said you can go now   Aunty Pat said.

10. My favourite book is Harry Potter and the Philosopher's Stone, what's yours he asked.

9.2 Hyphens

Sometimes hyphens are used when a prefix is added to a word. Hyphens need to be placed between a prefix and the root word in the following situations:
- To avoid confusion with another word.
  For example: re-formed means to be made again, while reformed means to be changed for the better.
  Another example is: re-sign means to sign again, while resign means to quit your job or position.
- When a prefix ending with a vowel is joined to a word starting with a vowel.
  For example: co-ordinate.
- When a prefix is followed by a word starting with a capital letter.
  For example: pre-Roman.
- When a prefix is followed by a year or date.
  For example: pre-1800.
- After the prefix self.
  For example: self-control.

Other uses of hyphens include:
- Wring the numbers twenty-one to ninety-nine as well as fractions.
  For example: forty-six or one-third.
- When turning a verb and adverb or preposition into a noun.
  For example: break-in or get-together.
- When writing compound words made up of a noun and an adjective.
  For example: sugar-free or accident-prone.
- When two nouns are used to make a verb.
  For example: to ice-skate.
- A compound word consisting of two nouns may be written with or without the hyphen.
  For example: playgroup and play-group are both correct.

If adding a hyphen makes the meaning clear, then a hyphen should be used.
The sentence: "I have six monthly appointments."
Could mean either:
I have six monthly-appointments.   or
I have six-monthly appointments.

Exercise 9.2
Add hyphens, if needed, to the following sentences.

1. She needed a chest x ray.

2. They had been married for fifty four years when she died.

3. There was a break in at the local shopping centre.

4. Post 1900 there has been a national education system in England.

5. For sale: a little used boat. (The boat is little but used a lot)

6. He appeared stern but was actually a warm hearted man.

7. He's a two year old child.

8. Please fasten your seat belt.

9. They had a second hand cabinet in the lounge room.

10. She needed to buy a present for her mother in law's birthday.

Find the punctuation mistake in the sentences below. Write the letter of that part of the sentence on the space to the left. If there is no mistake, write 'N'.

1. It was finally holiday's and he was looking forward to sleeping in.   __

A	B	C	D	E	F

2. He pleaded, "can I come too? The party will be so much fun."   __

A	B	C	D	E	F

3. The sun was just rising when he took the dog for a walk.   __

A	B	C	D	E

4. The families favourite food was Chinese. They did not have it often.   __

A	B	C	D	E

5. She has her piano lesson on wednesday, every week at 4:00 p.m.   __

A	B	C	D	E

6. Whats your favourite sandwich? My favourite is chicken and salad.   __

A	B	C	D	E	F

7. The tears began to roll down Zionas cheeks, first slowly then quickly.   __

A	B	C	D	E

8. Its known that Alexander the Great was born in July, 356 BC.   __

A	B	C	D	E

9. She walked as quickly as she could, She was worried it would be too late. __

A	B	C	D	E

10. She had: orange, blue and green pencils, blue and black pens and a ruler. __

A	B	C	D	E	F

Chapter 10: Word Sounds

10.1 Rhyming

Two words rhyme when their last syllable sounds the same. They may or may not be spelled the same.

Example: bite, night, sight and mite all rhyme.

In a half-rhyme the final consonant sound is the same but not the final vowel sound.

Example: build and child do not rhyme but are half-rhymes.

Exercise 10.1

Underline the word that does not rhyme with the others.

1. hair   bear   fear   care   their

2. rhyme   limb   time   lime   climb

3. clown   town   frown   own   down

4. fasten   listen   ten   bison   hasten

5. they   dismay   grey   neigh   sigh

Write the word that rhymes with the word on the left and completes the sentence.

6. OFF   The farmer put the animals' food in their _____.

7. CROW   He went to the party _____ he had a lot to do.

8. FULL   She applied the antiseptic using cotton _____.

9. GEESE   Can I please have a _____ of pizza?

10. GO   The cold and the _____ kept them from going outside.

10.2 Alliteration

Alliteration is the repetition of the consonant sound at the start of words, that are close together. They do not need to be spelled the same.
Example: **Ph**illip **ph**ones a **f**riend on **F**riday.

Many tongue twisters use alliteration.
Example: She sells sea shells by the sea-shore.

Alliteration helps to produce rhythm in a piece of writing. It can also help produce imagery and provide emphasis. Example: the slithering snake, or she had twinkle toes.

Exercise 10.2
Underline the words that alliterate in the sentences below.

1. Claire found the custard creams and crispy cookies in the cupboard.

2. Mike meandered through the magical moist night air.

3. Yesterday, we went on a trip to Windsor, he whispered.

4. Charlie cooked crunchy cream candies with a chocolate filling.

5. Her circus skills sent shivers up my spine.

Complete the unfinished words below, using alliteration.

6. The snake slithered over the slippery _ t _ n _ _

7. After the phone call, Fred _ _ _ w home.

8. They rescued and then _ _ _ r _ _ two rare rabbits.

9. They were pretty excited as they _ _ _ p _ _ _ _ for the party.

10. Dave has decided to _ _ _ v _ back home.

10.3 Assonance

Assonance is the repetition of a vowel sound.

Example: A h**o**st of golden daff**o**dils (from Wordsworth).

Assonance can be used to set the mood in poetry. Assonance of long vowel sounds tend to slow down the pace, making it sadder or more serious; while assonance of short vowel sounds can have the opposite effect.

Exercise 10.3

Underline the words that show assonance below.

1. Its wings grew and grew, until it flew and flew.

2. It's a deal, read the sheet and leave the room.

3. The cow found the meadow ground hard.

4. Try to light the fire, before nightfall.

5. He felt depressed and restless.

6. I looked here, there and everywhere.

7. I have an inkling it is an imp.

8. The beast rose from the sea to seek a feast.

9. One man went to sow and then mow a meadow.

10. Though frail she trailed through the glade.

10.4 Consonance

Consonance is the repetition of a consonant sound, particularly the consonant sound at the end of words.

Example: Goo**d** or kin**d**, I di**d** not fin**d**.

Consonance gives a sense of a beat and can help to convey speed.

Exercise 10.4

Underline the words that show consonance below.

1. It is the ideal sound file for the dial tone.
2. The light helped the plant to grow upright.
3. The black sack is in the back.
4. From dawn to sun down.
5. He was a good golfer with a strong swing.
6. I hear the pitter patter of little feet.
7. Her shoes clopped on the hard wood floor.
8. The hiker got near the moor.
9. The mash potatoes were on the dish.
10. The storm caused the animals to worm their way underground.

10.5 Onomatopoeia

Onomatopoeia is a word that sounds like its meaning.
Examples: meow, honk, book, smash and cuckoo

Onomatopoeia makes writing more expressive.

Exercise 10.5

Underline the words that show onomatopoeia below.

1. The young boys whizzed past on their shiny bicycles.

2. Be careful not to bump your head on the doorway.

3. Please, cover your mouth when you cough.

4. The croaking of the frogs kept her awake.

5. They enjoyed toasting marshmallows over the cackling fire.

6. The creak of the door let them know he was home.

7. He murmured the answer quietly under his breath.

8. She loved the sound of the leaves rustling in the wind.

9. He zipped up his sleeping bag, so he was toasty and warm.

10. Please, try not to pop the balloons.

Chapter 11: Word Structure

11.1 Silent letters

Many words have silent letters; letters that are written but not pronounced.
Examples: thumb, knife, foreign, island

Exercise 11.1

Underline the word that is spelled incorrectly and write it correctly on the line.

1. It was a long clime from the bottom.   _____

2. It was a very serious and solem occasion.   _____

3. Keep your receit in case you want a refund.   _____

4. This is the 42nd year of the Queen's rein.   _____

5. He chose a rap for lunch, instead of a sandwich.   _____

6. Always lisen to your parents.   _____

7. The coir sung beautifully at Christmas.   _____

8. I will assine you to groups.   _____

9. Her grandmother nitted her a nice warm jumper.   _____

10. The church was bilt in the 12th century.   _____

11.2 Palindromes and other backward words

A palindrome is a word (or phrase) that is spelled the same when written forwards and backwards.
Example: repaper (to cover again with paper).
It is possible to have phrases or sentences that are palindromes.
For example: "Was it a car or a cat I saw?"

Exercise 11.2

Underline the palindrome in the rows below.

1. madam   medal   middle   maxim
2. flat   level   fluff   lull
3. pulp   pear   pebble   peep
4. canoe   colic   kayak   kiosk
5. modern   minim   maxim   medium

In the following words, underline the word which when written backwards spells a word.

6. flick   tide   growth   cloud
7. knock   knits   ticks   stars
8. dearest   devilled   desserts   gram
9. smear   singer   slope   smart
10. stang   ghost   gongs   drops

11.3 Unstressed syllables

In some words a syllable does not receive much stress or emphasis. Often in this syllable the vowel sound is not pronounced or is indistinct.

Example: the word business is normally pronounced as if there is no 'i'.

Exercise 11.3

Underline the incorrectly spelled word and write it correctly on the line.

1. I thought the talk was very intresting.   _____

2. The performance was wonderfal.   _____

3. The letter was in the envolope.   _____

4. Look up the spelling in the dictonry.   _____

5. Do I have to move? I'm very comfertable.   _____

Put the correct vowels in the spaces below.

6. The gold_n ring is very valu_ble.

7. He is an exception_l student, bright and kind.

8. I am conf_d_nt that you are capable of doing well.

9. I need to get a cal_nd_r for next year.

10. Can you find a s_lution to the probl_m?

11.4 Anagrams

An anagram is a word where all the letters have been put in a different order.
Example: the anagram of **wolves** is **vowels**.

Sometimes the letters may be mixed but not make a word.
Example: DROW can be rearranged to word.

Exercise 11.4

Rearrange the letters of the word on the left to go with the definition.

1. ARTICLE   A musical performance.   _____

2. CASE   A pack of cards has four of these.   _____

3. THICKEN   A room in a house.   _____

4. VOTES   Used to cook.   _____

5. RENTAL   Found on the head of male deer.   _____

6. ROASTING   Plays a type of instrument.   _____

7. WEST   A winter dish, sometimes eaten with
                  dumplings.   _____

8. WHAT   When food is frozen you need to do this.   _____

9. RISEN   Emergency vehicles have one of these.   _____

10. BELOW   Part of the arm.   _____

Chapter 12: Synonyms

12.1 Synonyms

A synonym is a word that means the same or nearly the same.

There are two types of synonym question in the 11 plus exam: choosing the correct word or filling in the missing letters.

This type of question features heavily in C.E.M. exam papers.

Exercise 12.1

Choose the synonym of the word on the left.

1. **lazy**   idle   slow   difficult   fatigue

2. **calm**   tumult   tranquil   sleeping   tendency

3. **beginner**   new   haughty   feeble   novice

4. **forbid**   irate   inept   prohibit   insolent

5. **regret**   reconcile   remorse   recede   robust

6. **fair**   partial   biased   evened   just

7. **agree**   like   cherish   concur   abode

8. **affluent**   abundant   prosperous   shrewd   optimist

9. **diligent**   honourable   hardworking   funny   charming

10. **impromptu**   spontaneous   artificial   elaborate   fastidious

Exercise 12.2

Fill in the letters of the incomplete word to make a synonym of the word on the left. The word must be spelled correctly.

1. **weak**   f _ _ _ _ e
2. **empty**   v _ _ _ _ t
3. **normal**   u s _ _ _
4. **capacity** v o _ _ _ e
5. **also**   b e _ _ _ _ s
6. **funny**   h i _ _ _ _ _ _ u s
7. **serious**   s o _ _ _ _
8. **flower**   b l _ _ _ _ _
9. **allow**   p _ _ _ _ t
10. **defend**   p r _ _ _ _ t

Exercise 12.3

Choose the synonym of the word on the left.

1. **bewildered**   bedlam   confused   vaguely   vaccine
2. **pacify**   stalwart   jocular   reserved   placate
3. **important**   irrelevant   essential   complete   superficial
4. **aloof**   distant   deliver   impair   deplete
5. **demand**   inflate   require   consist   conclude
6. **conceal**   find   reveal   mask   under
7. **freight**   fright   fear   cargo   obscure
8. **tale**   animal   fable   moral   sketch
9. **respect**   esteem   sincere   frank   earnest
10. **droop**   fall   sink   sag   diminish

Exercise 12.4

Fill in the letters of the incomplete word to make a synonym of the word on the left. The word must be spelled correctly.

1. **plentiful**   a b _ _ _ _ n t

2. **able**   _ _ _ _ e t e n t

3. **leave**   a b _ _ _ _ n

4. **sudden**   a _ _ _ p t

5. **annoyance**   n _ _ _ _ _ c e

6. **anger**   w _ _ _ h

7. **boastful**   v _ _ _

8. **choice**   _ _ _ i o n

9. **destroy**   d e _ _ _ _ s h

10. **sturdy**   r o b _ _ _

Chapter 13: Antonyms

13.1 Antonyms

An antonym is a word that means the opposite or nearly the opposite.

As with synonyms there are two types of antonym questions: choosing the correct word or filling in the missing letters.

This type of questions also features heavily in the CEM exams.

Exercise 13.1

Choose the antonym of the word on the left.

1. **supporter**   opponent   advocate   advisor   match

2. **calculate**   exact   estimate   compute   evaluate

3. **transparent**   clear   transport   copious   opaque

4. **strict**   serious   grumpy   lenient   dawdle

5. **kindness**   disturb   malice   displease   cease

6. **sincere**   phony   vulnerable   friction   shrewd

7. **central**   permanent   quaint   peripheral   hesitant

8. **reluctant**   hesitant   eager   splurge   entrap

9. **unconcerned**   albeit   negotiate   fear   anxious

10. **upset**   misery   unique   stabilise   emotion

Exercise 13.2

Fill in the missing letters to form the antonym of the word on the left.

1. **simple**   c o _ _ _ _ x

2. **adult**   j u _ _ _ _ l e

3. **fresh**   s t _ _ _

4. **lead**   _ _ _ l o w

5. **work**   l e _ _ _ _ e

6. **abundant**   s c _ _ _ _

7. **forgive**   b l _ _ _

8. **kind**   _ _ _ e l

9. **wealth**   p o _ _ _ _ y

10. **graceful** c _ _ _ s y

Exercise 13.3

Choose the antonym of the word on the left.

1. **interesting**   fascinating   board   dull   fatigue

2. **passive**   flexible   weak   rough   active

3. **provoke**   soothe   encourage   insult   invoke

4. **drought**   deftly   drenching   moist   forest

5. **preserve**   jam   jar   transform   justify

6. **consider**   think   sublime   dismiss   divulge

7. **occupy**   habitat   vacate   vacant   vapour

8. **inscrutable**   understandable   petrify   tidy   mysterious

9. **correct**   right   edit   retort   erroneous

10. **undermine**   impede   remove   quarry   enhance

Exercise 13.4

Fill in the missing letters to form the antonym of the word on the left.

1. reckless   c a _ _ _ _ l
2. proud   a s _ _ _ _ d
3. calm   c _ _ _ t i c
4. arrogant   h _ _ _ _ e
5. compliment   i n _ _ _ t
6. divide   u n _ _ _
7. common   u n _ _ _ _
8. hero   v i _ _ _ _ n
9. tragic   c _ _ _ c
10. sunny   c l _ _ _ _

Chapter 14: Word Associations

14.1 Word associations - type

In this type of question you need to choose the word that is associated with the word on the left.

One way it may be associated is by type; that is the answer on the right fits into the category given on the left.

Example:

mammal   robin   dog   lizard   cod   snake

The answer is dog, because a dog is a mammal.

Exercise 14.1
Underline the word which is most closely associated with the word on the left.

1.	**building**	field	hall	guides	cupboard
2.	**tool**	scissors	wrench	driver	pen
3.	**fruit**	potato	tomato	carrot	spinach
4.	**colour**	apple	daffodil	rose	parsley
5.	**citrus**	banana	melon	lime	persimmon
6.	**reptile**	whale	frog	axolotl	crocodile
7.	**shoe**	sock	brogue	duffel	crimper
8.	**nocturnal**	bat	cat	bear	meerkat
9.	**tree**	larch	drey	aster	crocus
10.	**stationery**	memory	spoon	desk	envelope

14.2 Word associations - parts

Another type of word association question is when the answer is a part of the word on the left, or the word on the left is a part of the answer.
Example:

school   kitchen   classroom   bedroom   temple

While some schools are boarding so do have bedrooms (normally called dormitories or dorms) they are not specific to schools, classroom is most closely associated with schools, so classroom is the answer.

This type can also include occupations and where they work.
Example:

office   teacher   pilot   miner   secretary

The answer is secretary.

Exercise 14.2
Underline the word which is most closely associated to the word on the left.

1. **hospital**   people   large   cafe   radiographer

2. **encyclopaedia** history   fashion   articles   people

3. **paragraph**   cards   writing   sentence   court

4. **canal**   boat   barge   steamer   yacht

5. **botany**   bathroom   money   drawing   biology

6. **tines**   elude   fork   pencil   radio

7. **laboratory**   scientist optician   actuary   judge

8. **organism**   book   folder   cell   court

9. **miner**   desk   fork   quarry   ship

10. **building**   rain   men   work   brick

14.3 Word associations - other

There are many other ways that words can be associated. A few of them are:
- something that is used somewhere or in something eg. athletics, track.
- something that is the same shape eg. sphere, ball.
- synonyms.
- something that matches the words meaning eg. gigantic, whale.
- something that is needed or used in an activity eg. knitting, wool.
- something that you do with an item eg. set, table.
- two things that go together eg salt and pepper or bread and butter.
- how something is made eg. weave, fabric.

Exercise 14.3
Underline the word which is most closely associated to the word on the left.

1. **cuboid**	square	box	build	net
2. **mop**	ceiling	wall	floor	pole
3. **shuttlecock**	mood	squash	darts	badminton
4. **ladle**	tennis	soup	shoe	quiche
5. **grief**	joy	loss	find	stars
6. **minute**	fast	cat	bacteria	yoghurt
7. **scales**	amphibian	reptile	shark	stingray
8. **oil**	duck	plain	rig	fill
9. **bread**	seep	credit	cake	toast
10. **diurnal**	day	night	change	twice

Chapter 15: Odd One Out

15.1 Odd One Out - meaning

Odd one out questions involve finding the word that does not belong. You need to find what is the same about all the words, but one.

Example: violin   flute   clarinet   oboe   piccolo

All of them are woodwind instruments except violin, so violin is the odd one out.

Exercise 15.1

Underline the word which is the odd one out.

1. Thailand, Vietnam, Mexico, Tokyo, Canada

2. banana, apple, grape, pear, potato

3. heart, stomach, neck, liver, lungs

4. pen, paper, pencil, crayon, chalk

5. pool, lake, pond, water, swamp

6. Earth, Moon, Mars, Saturn, Venus

7. November, October, January, July, December

8. hail, rain, wind, snow, sleet

9. Africa, China, France, India, Australia

10. anger, ire, furious, fury, pacify

15.2 Odd One Out – Word Structure

While most odd one out questions focus on the meaning of words, some involve looking at the structure of words. Only look at the structure if there is no connection with the meaning of the words.

Some of the ways word structure may be the same include:
- rhyming
- containing the same letters or letter combinations
- silent letters
- palindromes
- alliteration

Exercise 15.2

Underline the word which is the odd one out.

1. flop, phone, feather, pills, from

2. madam, level, modern, kayak, minim

3. plough, cow, bough, vow, know

4. stab, climb, lamb, limb, tomb

5. transit, tailed, traffic, tropics, trapped

6. right, kite, eight, height, mite

7. plates, staple, slept, petals, pastel

8. relit, straw, mined, deliver, sword

9. roar, fore, coal, door, bore

10. letter, sooner, staff, weakly, cellar

Chapter 16: Homophones

16.1 Homophones

Homophone comes from the Greek *homos* meaning 'same' and *phonos* meaning 'sound'. So homophone literally means 'same sound' and are words that sound the same but are spelled differently.

These words often feature in cloze exercises, where you are required to choose the correct form of the word.

Exercise 16.1
Choose the correct form of the homophone in the sentences below.

1. As her son had already gone, it was only (fair, fare) that she took her daughter to the (fair, fare).

2. He (saw, soar, sore) that the (saw, soar, sore) must be very (saw, soar, sore).

3. Can you please (lessen, lesson) the volume of noise in the (lessen, lesson).

4. There is a small (flaw, floor) in the wood of the (flaw, floor).

5. I was not (allowed, aloud) to talk (allowed, aloud) in class.

6. The (principal, principle) objective is to stay true to my (principals, principles).

7. He had some pet chickens and other (foul, fowl) though his neighbour thought they were quite (foul, fowl).

8. The (morning, mourning) car took them to the funeral, yesterday (morning, mourning).

9. Ke needed more (flower, flour) to make a nice (moose, mousse) for dessert.

10. She paid him a (complement, compliment) on passing his driving (licence, license).

Exercise 16.2

Write a homophone of the word on the left in the space provided.

1. ISLE   He walked down the _____ containing tinned fruit but forgot to pick up pineapple.

2. COURSE   The sandpaper was very _____.

3. IDOL   He was very _____ with little to do.

4. POOR   Can you _____ yourself a drink?

5. AIR   He was the _____ to the throne.

6. SIDE   He _____ heavily, when he heard the bad news.

7. MARE   The local _____ visited the school.

8. LED   The roof was lined with _____.

9. BARON   The land was very _____ with almost no vegetation.

10. EARN   The used a large _____ to make the hot drinks.

Chapter 17: Homographs

17.1 Word Links

Homograph comes from the Greek *homos* meaning same and *grapho* meaning 'write.' Homographs are words with the same spelling but with more than one meaning. They may be pronounced differently depending on context.

Example: the word 'rock' can mean both a stone or to sway back and forth.

'Rock' sounds the same with both meanings.

The word 'minute' can mean 60 seconds or very small.

The sound of 'minute' changes according to the meaning.

The main use of homographs in the 11 plus exam is in word links. In word links you need to choose which word can go with two different sets of words.

Example: (paste, glue) (twig, branch)

Answer: stick

The answer is "stick" because to stick a worksheet in your book is the same as to glue it in and a stick can be part of a tree like a twig or a branch.

Exercise 17.1

Underline the word which goes with both sets of words below.

1. (material, contain) (happy, satisfied)
    pleased, glad, joyous, placid, content.

2. (allow, let) (ticket, warrant)
    authorise, enable, pass, permit, voucher

3. (alphabet, word) (postcard, note)
    letter, character, symbol, stamp, message

4. (thin, delicate) (well, good)
    excellent, healthy, bright, fine, fragile

5. (music, melody) (adjust, correct)
    song, tune, aria, piece, change

6. (learn, revise) (investigate, survey)
    study, work, article, essay, report

7. (guide, head) (copper, iron)
    conduct, lead, promote, metal, tin

8. (sphere, globe) (disco, party)
    Earth, orb, ball, gathering, social

9. (rip, shred) (cry, weep)
    tear, split, cut, slash, snag

10. (leg, hand) (metre, inch)
    foot, wrist, arm, stone, mile

Exercise 17.2

Underline the word which goes with both sets of words below.

1. (step, tread) (sticker, emboss)
   trample, stomp, trudge, label, stamp

2. (fall, submerge) (basin, bowl)
   drop, sink, descend, pool, gulf

3. (obscene, curse) (promise, vow)
   swear, profanity, declare, state, pronounce

4. (bitter, tangy) (quiche, flan)
   acidic, tart, sharp, pastry, strudel

5. (near, far) (shut, slam)
   adjacent, join, connect, open, close

6. (fire, lighter) (equal, replica)
   match, kindle, ignite, copy, peer

7. (endure, tolerate) (cat, horse)
   accept, withstand, dog, lion, bear

8. (watch, check) (television, screen)
   observe, supervise, examine, monitor, display

9. (tree, twig) (quack, roar)
   stink, trunk, howl, miaow, bark

10. (up, across) (feathers, fur)
    down, left, right, wool, pile

Chapter 18: Compound Words

18.1 Compound words

In this type of question, choose one word from each group to make a new word.

The word formed must be correctly spelled.
Example: (lips, leg, arm) (stick, tick, tock)
lips & stick does not make a word, but lips & tick does, as lipstick has only one 's.'

Exercise 18.1

Choose one word from each group to make a new correctly spelled word.

1. (else, end, entry)   (when, where, what)

2. (an, be, on)   (case, cause, slow)

3. (in, out, to)   (go, part, day)

4. (fast, but, rat)   (ten, tin, ton)

5. (cram, pick, sauce)   (pan, pen, pin)

6. (for, fort, fought)   (nite, knight, night)

7. (for, fore, fort)   (grow, give, glare)

8. (step, key, door)   (lock, hole, pen)

9. (arm, leg, wood)   (mix, chair, den)

10. (clip, cut, heart)   (lit, beet, let)

18.2 Compound word families

Many compound words can be made from the same word.
Example: footage, football, footbridge, foothill, footman, footprint, footpath, footstep and footwork are all compound words made using the word 'foot'.

Exercise 18.2

Find the word that can be placed in front of all the words below and write it on the line.

1. __ache, __ground, __pack, __date _____

2. __arm, __place, __proof, __work _____

3. __more, __place, __where, __thing _____

4. __grow, __side, __let, __door _____

5. __cup, __cake, __spoon, __house _____

6. __get, __give, __bid, __age _____

7. __ache, __light, __band, __line _____

8. __bag, __bank, __castle, __paper _____

9. __bell, __mat, __man, __step _____

10. __land, __pile, __wind, __work _____

18.3 One word from two

Often compound words neither sound like the words they came from nor take their meaning from the original words.

Example: he + art = heart

Heart does not sound like 'he' and 'art'; the meaning of heart has nothing to do with drawing pictures or the male pronoun.

Exercise 18.3

Choose one word from each group to make a new correctly spelled word.

1. (hand, foot, toe) (sum, some, son)

2. (cat, rat, cot) (tin, far, her)

3. (at, be, so) (in, on, it)

4. (he, she, her) (at, eat, in)

5. (dam, dip, pin) (fore, pick, age)

6. (inn, is, on) (land, self, too)

7. (past, mass, fore) (wry, tee, age)

8. (wheat, rough, now) (her, here, ten)

9. (air, err, ledge) (and, her, son)

10. (sat, port, bud) (tin, tray, get)

Chapter 19: Which word

19.1 Crossword definitions

In these questions complete the word to match the definition.

Exercise 19.1

1. A n _ _ _ _ m   A word which means the opposite.

2. c h a _ _ _ _ e r   A person in a story.

3. p l a _ _ _ _ m   A train leaves from one.

4. p i _ _ _   Flies a plane.

5. e c _ _ _ _ e   When the Earth, moon and Sun all line up.

6. e _ _ _ _ r a t e   To change from a liquid to a gas.

7. f i _ _ _ _   Changes frequently.

8. q u _ _ _   A question.

9. s a _ _ _ _ c h   Often eaten for lunch.

10. v o _ _ _ _ l e   A liquid that evaporates easily is this. Also a person who becomes angry easily.

19.2 Words within words

In these questions a few letters have been left out of a longer word. These missing letters spell a word. To answer first work out what the full word should be and then which letters are missing. Finally check that these letters make a word.

Example: He loved playing games on his COMER.

The full word should be COM<u>PUT</u>ER
but we already have   COM   ER
So the missing letters are PUT, which is a word.

Exercise 19.2

Find the word of three or four letters missing from the word in capitals. Write the missing word on the line.

1. She enjoyed wearing JEERY to parties.   _____

2. He really STGLED to learn his times tables.   _____

3. You must listen to your TER.   _____

4. She put all her appointments on the CAAR.   _____

5. The house was decorated with lots of Christmas ORNTES.   _____

6. Please be CFUL not to hurt yourself.   _____

7. Difficult questions are more of a CHENGE.   _____

8. During the workshop there were lots of different IVITIES. _____

9. Please be nice, I don't want an ARENT.   _____

10. SOIMES we need to accept change.   _____

Chapter 20: Mixed-up Sentences

20.1 Swap Two Words

In these questions you need to underline the two words that need to swap places for the sentence to make sense.

To do this:

1. Read the sentence slowly.
2. Decide which two words are in the wrong position.
3. Re-read the sentence back to yourself in your head.

Example: All capital start with a sentences letter.

The sentence should read: All **sentences** start with a **capital** letter.

So, the answer is capital and sentences.

Exercise 20.1
Underline the two words which should swap places in the sentences below.

1. A picture is words a thousand worth.

2. He enjoyed holidays in on the sleeping.

3. You should complete your all homework.

4. England is the capital of London.

5. Thomas went to cinema the last week.

6. I never imagined that a moment for I would win.

7. When heated and liquid will evaporate a become a gas.

8. The clown frightened girl little the and she ran off screaming.

9. The huge stand was a lemonade success.

10. His forgot to hand in the last page of he homework.

20.2 Rearranging Sentences

Sometimes more than two words are rearranged.

Exercise 20.2
Rearrange the words below to make a sensible sentence.

1. train here should soon be the

_____

2. test studying are they a have tomorrow they because

_____

3. tomorrow is birthday her party evening

_____

4. postcard sent my me parents a

_____

5. taller older children get grow as they

_____

6. the the the day zoo at loved children

_____

7. started that wonder who I rumour

_____

8. he he his hurt fell when hand

_____

9. very little we snow this had winter

_____

10. fluently speaks languages she three

_____

Chapter 21: Sentences with an Extra Word

21.1 Extra Word

The most common type of question involving "mixed-up sentences" or "jumbled sentences" in the C.E.M. exam is where all the words can be used to make a sentence except one. The answer to the question is the extra word.

Be careful, with some questions it is possible to make a sentence with all but two words. In this case look for a different sentence that uses all but one word.

Example: reading eating spent he the a book evening

All the words but one can be rearranged to make the sentence:
He spent the evening reading a book.
The word not used is **eating**. So, the answer is eating.

Exerices 21.1
In the following questions all the words but one can be used to make a sentence.
Which word is not used?

   1. cancelled match rain was of because as the   _____

   2. tired further was he and not see walk any could   _____

   3. only of had cake piece some I little a   _____

   4. bird tree wings was the the singing in   _____

   5. Tom not alarm person a morning is   _____

   6. wash hands cooking bathroom should your you before you start

                                                    _____

7. garden flowers the dog hole a dug in the   _____

8. winter the trees many leaves lose their in snow   _____

9. I card library the the book borrowed from   _____

10. go walk along for he would often fish a the river   _____

Exercise 21.2

In the following questions all the words but one can be used to make a sentence. Which word is not used?

1. finished she all night last book the reading   _____

2. going they on seaside holiday are tomorrow   _____

3. everywhere found him looked we couldn't but find   _____

4. here left car they an so will hour soon ago be   _____

5. the dangerous snakes although some most are are harmless_____

6. morning clown laughing children the were the at   _____

7. bus came school he had to by today   _____

8. the desk is pen there a on of   _____

9. very studies exams clever he is hard and   _____

10. documentaries population he wildlife watching loves   _____

Chapter 22: Cloze - meaning

22.1 Cloze – making sense

There are two types of cloze in the 11 Plus: missing words and missing letters.

Firstly, a cloze question needs to make sense.

If you have time, you should read through the sentence or passage to ensure that it makes sense.

Example: The doctor (prescribed, checked, practiced) the patient some (sandwiches, medicine, diet).

Answer: prescribed, medicine

Full sentence: The doctor **prescribed** the patient some **medicine**.
This is the only combination that makes sense.

Exercise 22.1
Underline the best word in each set of brackets below.

Animals are [1](stratified, classified, designated) into different groups depending on their [2](features, profile, hallmark). Vertebrates are animals with a backbone or spine. One class of vertebrates are mammals. Mammals have [3](hare, hair, fluff) or fur covering their body and feed their young milk. Only two mammals lay eggs. Mammals are endothermic. This means they [4](static, constant, control) their body temperature through internal means. The only other group of animals which are endothermic [5](was, is, or) birds. This has [6](caused, enabled, resulted) mammals to [7](populate, consume, live) in almost every climate on Earth. Other [8](feature, characteristics, choices) of mammals include [9](have, has, having) lungs to [10](inhalation, breath, breathe) and sweat glands. Mammals range in size from the 30-40 mm bumble bee bat to the 33 metre long blue whale.

22.2 Cloze - Homophones

In cloze exercises be careful to choose the correct homophone for the passage to make sense.

Example: "What should I (ware, wear, where)?" asked Ziona.

Answer: wear

Exercise 22.2
Underline the correct word in each set of brackets below.

The road [1](their, there, they're) was in bad repair. They were worried that they might damage a [2](tire, tyre, try) on a [3](captivity, hole, whole). As [4](day, knight, night) deepened and darkness descended their concern grew. Struggling to [5](sea, see, saw) in the moonlight they [6](wandered, wondered, wonder) about stopping until morning. They had [7](heard, herd, knew) of others who had had an accident. Showing [8](grate, great, greet) care they edged forward slowly. Finally the road widened, became [9](strait, straight, windy) and the [10](reign, rein, rain) lifted. The trip became much more pleasant and they soon arrived safely and all lived happily every after.

Chapter 23: Cloze - Grammar

23.1 Cloze – Grammar

In cloze exercises it is important that the passage is grammatically correct.

Things to look out for include:

- correct type of word, eg. noun, verb.
- verbs in correct tense.
- 'an' not 'a' before vowels.

Remember, 'could of' and 'would of' are never correct but should be 'could have' or 'would have.'

Also remember that 'I done' is incorrect and should be 'I did' or 'I have done.'

Exercise 23.1
Underline the correct word in each set of brackets below.

It should [1](have, of, was) been a special day. It started [2](good, great, well) with the sun shining and a clear blue sky. Rizak [3](open, opens, opened) his eyes [4](quick, slowly, now) thinking of the day stretched [5](front, out, over) before him. He had never [6](been, went, visited) to the zoo before and he was [7](extremely, little, lots) excited. Finally after packing lunch and plenty of water they were off. Unfortunately there was an [8](collision, jam, accident) on the way which caused a long delay. Then they heard on the radio that the zoo was closed due to the lions [9](antics, escaped, escaping). So they turned back and hoped to go [10](another, other, soon) day.

23.2 Cloze – Meaning, Homophones and Grammar

When doing cloze questions the following things need to be considered:

- Meaning
- Spelling
- Grammar

Exercise 23.2
Underline the correct word in each set of brackets below.

The Himalayas [1](are, is, was) a mountain range [2](locality, location, situated) in South Asia, spanning five countries: Nepal, India, China, Bhutan and Pakistan. The largest mountain in the Himalayas is Mount Everest, with a [3](height, high, altitude) of 8848 metres [4](above, higher, near) sea level.

Three of the world's major rivers [5](initiate, originate, begun) in the Himalayas: the Indus, the Ganges and the Brahmaputra.

The Himalayas with its [6](varied, variety, diverse) of altitude, rainfall and soil is home to a range of unique plants and animals. The Himalayas are home to over 300 species of mammal, many of them found nowhere else and some of them are threatened or [7](extinct, heritage, endangered). There is also an [8](estimated, about, approximate) 10 000 plant species, 3160 of which are [9](unusual, distributed, unique) to the area. However, while there are [10](close, nearly, endemic) 980 bird species only 15 are unique to the Himalayas.

23.3 Cloze – Word bank

Sometimes cloze exercises are presented with a word bank and you choose which word goes in which spot. Normally there are extra words in the word bank which are not used.

Exercise 23.3
Choose which word goes best in the spaces below, and write the letter of that word below.

Set 1.

reptile	fierce	myth	legendary	symbolises
A	B	C	D	E

reptilian	knight	feature	hieroglyph	over	around
F	G	H	I	J	K

Dragons are ___(1)___ creatures, normally with snake-like or ___(2)___ features. There are two separate traditions of the dragon, the European dragon and the Asian dragon. The European dragon tends to be ___(3)___ and breathe fire, while the Asian dragon, of which the Chinese is the most known, ___(4)___ power and luck. Dragons ___(5)___ in stories the world ___(6)___ .

1. _____

2. _____

3. _____

4. _____

5. _____

6. _____

arrive	attendance	come	sunny	arriving	operation
A	B	C	D	E	F

conundrum	commotion	palaver	route	incident
G	H	I	J	K

The three friends ventured to the park, as it was a __(7)__ day. On __(8)__ at the park they hid behind a large tree as there seemed to be quite a __(9)__ , with police and ambulance both in __(10)__ .

7. _____

8. _____

9. _____

10. _____

Chapter 24: Cloze – Missing Letters

24.1 Missing Letters

In this type of cloze work out what the missing word should be and then complete it.

Example: Robert shivered as he waited on the train pl _ _ _ o _ m.

The full word should be: platform.
So, the letters a,t,f,r are added to the spaces (and are the answer).

Exercise 24.1
Complete the words in the passage below.

Winter is the [1]se _ _ _ n when temperatures [2]d _ _ p. If it becomes cold [3]en _ _ _ h snow may [4]co _ _ _ the ground. This can be dangerous as ice forms and people may [5]s _ _ p. The roads can be particularly unsafe as people lose [6]co _ _ _ _ l of their cars and [7]_ _ _ idents occur. People need to find ways of keeping warm. Some may choose to stay inside with a [8]bl _ _ _ ng fire. Those who need to go outside wear coats, [9]sc _ _ _ _ s and gloves. A nice cup of hot [10]cho _ _ _ _ te always helps too.

24.2 Spelling and Homophones

In missing letter activities spelling is particularly important.

A few things to consider include:

- ie or ei.
- ice or ise.
- double letters.
- silent letters.

As with missing words it is important that the correct homophone is used.

Exercise 24.2
Complete the words in the passage below.

Although I have been told that I'm invited, I have not yet [1]re _ _ _ ved my

invitation. So, yesterday I [2]che _ _ _ d with my [3]n _ _ _ _ bours to see if it

had come with [4]th _ _ _   mail. Nevertheless, I went shopping for a

[5]sui _ _ _ _ e outfit. I found it very [6]valu _ _ _ e to have a friend come with

me and provide another [7]op _ _ _ _ n. I found something that is very [8]comfort

_ _ _ _ but still looks [9]eleg _ _ _. I am now looking forward to this grand

[10]oc _ _ _ _ on

Chapter 25: Comprehension – Types of Text

25.1 Introduction to Comprehension.

Comprehension is the understanding and interpretation of what is read.

There are two types of text:

1. **Prose** - Written in sentences and paragraphs.

   Example: Once upon a time in a land of verdant, green hills lived a young lad, whose strength was increasing.

2. **Poetry** - Normally written using rhythm and / or rhyme.

   Example:

   Up on the hills, over yonder,

   The lad grew stronger and stronger.

Prose can be either:

- **Fiction** – Made-up or pretend.

  Example: Suddenly, the four children found themselves in the fairy-kingdom. "You're here at last," breathed a fairy in quite magnificent clothes. "We have quite a situation here and really need your help."

- **Non-fiction** – True.

  Example: England is a country covering 130,395 km². It is part of the United Kingdom and on the Western side of Europe. England has a population of over 50 million people. The capital city is London.

There are many types of prose, including:

- **Narrative** – Tells a story, includes short stories, novels and biographies.

  A biography is the story of someone's life.

  An autobiography is the story of the author's life.

- **Journalism** - Provides information but can be biased.

  Includes magazines and newspapers.

- **Diaries and journals** - A series of events told in chronological order.

  Can be fiction or non-fiction.

- **Informative texts** - Imparts information. Does not tell a story.

  Includes dictionaries, encyclopaedias and text-books.

- **Speeches** - The narration of a speech.

  Can be fiction or non-fiction. Can stand on its own or be a part of a larger work.

- **Letters** - Communication by post or email. Can be formal or informal.

  Can be fiction or non-fiction. Many letters of famous people have been preserved.

- **Play-scripts** - Tells a story, with the character's dialogue.

  Includes the scripts of movies, plays, musicals and pantomimes.

- **Advertising** - A form of persuasive writing designed to get the reader to buy, think or act in a particular way.

Prose is written for one of four reasons:

1. To entertain.
2. To inform.
3. To persuade.
4. To preserve / remember.

It is very useful when deciding what type of text a piece of prose is, to determine whether it is subjective or objective. If it is objective is based on the facts while if it is subjective it includes opinion. A piece of writing can be described as biased if it favours one opinion, without giving equal worth to opposing opinions. Some types of writing such as letters, journalism and advertising are likely to show bias while informative texts are generally unbiased.

Exercise 24.1

State whether the following are prose or poetry, fiction or non-fiction:

1. There once was a man called Pat,
   Who doted on his pet rat.
   When asked if he'd have another,
   He said his rat had a brother,
   Who had been chased away by a cat.

   Prose / Poetry: _____
   Fiction / Non-fiction: _____

2. William Blake was an English painter, poet and printmaker. He was born in 1757, in Soho, London. Perhaps his best known work is the poem "Tyger." He died in August 1827.

   Prose / Poetry: _____
   Fiction / Non-fiction: _____

3. Waking with a large stretch, Douglas looked around. He couldn't really believe he was waking up in another world. Finally, the technology had come together and the civilisation on Mars had become a reality. He pinched himself just to check it was really true. The air scrubbers gave the air a metallic tang. He felt it in his nose. He knew from this alone that he was in an unusual environment. A space-station is never quiet. There are always people watching dials like hawks. As a slight difference in numbers could spell doom for all those inside.

   Prose / Poetry: _____
   Fiction / Non-fiction: _____

4. There's a very funny insect that you do not often spy,
And it isn't quite a spider, and it isn't quite a fly;
It is something like a beetle, and a little like a bee,
But nothing like a wooly grub that climbs upon a tree.
Its name is quite a hard one, but you'll learn it soon, I hope.
So try:
    Tri-
        Tri-anti-wonti-
            Triantiwontigongolope.

It lives on weeds and wattle-gum, and has a funny face;
Its appetite is hearty, and its manners a disgrace.
When first you come upon it, it will give you quite a scare,
But when you look for it again, you find it isn't there.
And unless you call it softly it will stay away and mope.
So try:
    Tri-
        Tri-anti-wonti-
            Triantiwontigongolope.

It trembles if you tickle it or tread upon its toes;
It is not an early riser, but it has a snubbish nose.
If you snear at it, or scold it, it will scuttle off in shame,
But it purrs and purrs quite proudly if you call it by its name,
And offer it some sandwiches of sealing-wax and soap.
So try:
    Tri-
        Tri-anti-wonti-
            Triantiwontigongolope .

But of course you haven't seen it; and I truthfully confess
That I haven't seen it either, and I don't know its address.
For there isn't such an insect, though there really might have been
If the trees and grass were purple, and the sky was bottle green.
It's just a little joke of mine, which you'll forgive, I hope.
Oh, try!
    Tri-
        Tri-anti-wonti-
            Triantiwontigongolope.

Prose / Poetry: _____

Fiction / Non-fiction: _____

What type of prose are the excerpts below?

5. In this grave hour, perhaps the most fateful in our history, I send to every household of my peoples, both at home and overseas, this message, spoken with the same depth of feeling for each one of you as if I were able to cross your threshold and speak to you myself.

For the second time in the lives of most of us we are at war.

Type of Prose: _____

Reason for writing: _____

6. STEEN. Supper! How could we forget supper?—Give me a big bowlful, Holger.

HOLGER. (Handing STEEN his porridge) There isn't a big bowlful here.

STEEN. (Taking the bowl and hugging it) Nice kind good supper, umh! (Begins to eat eagerly)

HOLGER. (Suddenly looking toward the door) Listen!

BERTEL. To what?

HOLGER. (Awed, hesitant) Someone—sobbing—at the door! (He goes to it, the others watching him startled, he opens the door, finds nothing, closes it and comes back) Nothing there!

BERTEL. The wind!—Thy old tricks, Holger,—always dreaming some strange thing.

HOLGER. (Recalled by BERTEL'S words to something else) Didst thou pass an old woman on the road—near here?

BERTEL. Not a soul nearer than the town gate. (HOLGER stands thinking, absorbed) Come, boy, eat,—eat! See how Steen eats!

Type of Prose: _____

Reason for writing: _____

7. Some of our maids sitting up late last night to get things ready against our feast today, Jane called up about three in the morning, to tell us of a great fire they saw in the City. So I rose, and slipped on my night-gown and went to her window, and thought it to be on the back side of Mark Lane at the farthest; but, being unused to such fires as followed, I thought it far enough off, and so went to bed again, and to sleep. . . . By and by Jane comes and tells me that she hears that above 300 houses have been burned down tonight by the fire we saw, and that it is now burning down all Fish Street, by London Bridge. So I made myself ready presently, and walked to the Tower; and there got up upon one of the high places, . . .and there I did see the houses at the end of the bridge all on fire, and an infinite great fire on this and the other side . . . of the bridge. . . . So down [I went], with my heart full of trouble, to the Lieutenant of the Tower, who tells me that it began this morning in the King's baker's house in Pudding Lane, and that it hath burned St. Magnus's Church and most part of Fish Street already. So I rode down to the waterside, . . . and there saw a lamentable fire. . . .

Type of Prose: _____

Reason for writing: _____

8. The Village of Eyam, in Derbyshire is often referred to "The Plague Village." In 1665 the village tailor George Viccars received a parcel of cloth from London that contained the Plague. Since the cloth was damp he hung it out to dry and released the fleas carrying the Plague. George Viccars became the first victim. However, the village decided that instead of evacuating they would remain within the confines of the village to minimize the spread of the disease to neighbouring areas. To minimize cross infection, food and other supplies were left outside the village, at either the Boundary Stones, or at Mompesson's Well, high above the village. Coins were left in vinegar to help disinfect the coins. The Plague in Eyam raged for 14 months and claimed the lives of at least 260 villagers. They had prevented the Plague from spreading to other towns, but many paid the ultimate price for their commitment.

Type of Prose: _____

Reason for writing: _____

9. The cyclone had set the house down, very gently for a cyclone in the midst of a country of marvellous beauty. There were lovely patches of green sward all about, with stately trees bearing rich and luscious fruits. Banks of gorgeous flowers were on every hand, and birds with rare and brilliant plumage sang and fluttered in the trees and bushes. ...

While she stood looking eagerly at the strange and beautiful sights, she noticed coming toward her a group of the queerest people she had ever seen. They were not as big as the grown folk she had always been used to; but neither were they very small. In fact, they seemed about as tall as Dorothy, who was a well-grown child for her age, although they were, so far as looks go, many years older.

Three were men and one a woman, and all were oddly dressed. ... "You are welcome, most noble Sorceress, to the land of the Munchkins. We are so grateful to you for having killed the wicked Witch of the East, and for setting our people free from bondage."

Type of Prose: _____

Reason for writing: _____

10. Our award-winning designs strip back unnecessary costs from the factory floor to your front room. Enabling you to get top quality furniture at a price you can afford.

Type of Prose: _____

Reason for writing: _____

Chapter 26: Comprehension – Reading the Text

26.1 Reading the text for meaning.

The first task in any comprehension exercise is to read the passage. It is imperative that you understand the overall meaning of the passage and the meaning of individual paragraphs. In C.E.M. Exams often time is relatively short, so it is important that the first reading is thorough.

One technique that is helpful for longer passages is to annotate the text as you read. For each paragraph write on or two words in the margin that summarise what the paragraph is about. This achieves two things: it forces you to work out the main point of the paragraphs as you read. Secondly, it acts as a set of bookmarks, so when you are answering a question you can very quickly go to the relevant part of the passage. When using this technique it is important **not** to write too much or reading through your notes will take as long as re-reading the passage.

Example:

dogs	Dogs are a very varied type of animal. All dogs are of the same species.
origin	All dogs originate from the wolf, the different breeds developing over centuries by selective breeding.

Read the passage below, then answer the questions that follow.

BOOKS

It has been said that "Whenever you read a good book, somewhere in the world a door opens to allow in more light." Books provide us with knowledge, empowerment, an escape and pure joy.

People have expressed themselves in spoken language and written form for millennia. From about 35 000 BC, Cro-Magnon man used language and cave-paintings to express concepts in everyday life and to tell stories.

However it was much later in Sumer, Mesopotamia (now in Iraq) and independently in Egypt that true writing emerged, around 3200 BC. In both places the writing system evolved from small images (pictograms) used as words, literally depicting the thing in question. But pictograms of this kind are limited and over time the systems developed into symbols, with symbols representing both concepts and sounds. In Sumer the Cuneiform script developed while in Egypt the Hieroglyphic system came into being. Much later the Chinese system seems to have been developed independently.

Initially, anything that could be written on was used for the purpose of writing. This included wood, metal, clay, stones, bone, shells and leaves. In Mesopotamia writing was principally written on clay tablets with a wedge-shaped stylus. In Egypt, papyrus was invented. Many stone tablets and fragments or sherds of pottery called ostraca have been found in archaeological digs. Sherds of pottery were often used in Egypt to make short notes, letters, receipts and for calculations.

Papyrus is a thin paper-like material made from the pith of the papyrus plant, a type of reed growing along the Nile River. Papyrus was written on using a fine reed pen. Papyrus allowed the development of the scroll. A scroll was normally divided up into pages. The scroll was usually unrolled so that one page was exposed at a time, for writing or reading, with the remaining pages rolled up either to the left and right or above and below the visible page. Some scrolls were simply rolled up pages, while others had wooden or ivory rollers on each end.

Along with the written script the material written on continued to be developed. Parchment progressively replaced papyrus. Its production began around the 3rd century BC. Made using the skins of animals (sheep, cattle, donkey, antelope, etc.), parchment proved easier to conserve over time; it was more solid, and allowed one to erase text. It was a very expensive medium because of the rarity of material and the time required to produce a document. Vellum is the parchment made from calf skin, lambskin or kidskin, as opposed to that from alder animals, however the finest quality of parchment was often referred to as vellum regardless of the type of animal skin used.

The scroll gradually gave way to the codex (plural: codices). A codex is a book made up of a number of sheets of paper, vellum, papyrus, or similar, with hand-written content, stacked and joined at one edge. The codex held several advantages over the scroll as it was more compact, it was easier to access a particular point rather than requiring access from beginning to end and both sides of the material could be written on. The codex began to replace the scroll almost as soon as it was invented. In Egypt by the fifth century, the codex outnumbered the scroll by ten to one based on surviving examples, and by the sixth century the scroll had almost vanished from use as a medium. Codices remained the main format for written material for centuries. While, technically modern paperbacks are codices, the term is now used only for manuscript (hand-written) books, which were produced from Late antiquity until the Middle Ages.

Books remained predominantly hand written and very expensive until the development of the printing press. The world's first movable type printing press technology was invented and developed in China by the Han Chinese printer Bi Sheng between the years 1041 and 1048 AD. However, it was the invention of movable type mechanical printing technology in Europe, which is credited to the German printer Johannes Gutenberg Press in 1450 that revolutionised books in the West. The Gutenberg enabled scientists, philosophers, politicians, and religious officials to replicate their ideas quickly, relatively cheaply and make them available to large audiences. Learning was revolutionised and books became available to the masses.

The development of the printing press defined the book for the next five hundred years. Recently, a new concept has been developed which is that of the electronic book, commonly referred to as the e-book. An e-book is a book-length publication in digital form, consisting of text, images, or both, readable on computers or other electronic devices. While many e-books are the digital form of a printed book, many e-books do not have a printed equivalent. The concept of the e-book dates back to the 1930s, with the first e-book completed in the 1970s. However, it is only since 2000 that the e-book has gained mass popularity. Conservative estimates now suggest that at least 30% of all book sales are e-books.

The history of the book is fascinating and has come a long way from the first pictures pained in caves by our ancestors. The development of the book through all these stages has enabled us to have access to a wealth of information and entertainment. The book continues to evolve with hyperlinks and videos already being embedded into some formats of e-book.

For each of the chapters in the above passage, state the main meaning of the passage in **only** one or two words.

Paragraph 1. _____

Paragraph 2. _____

Paragraph 3. _____

Paragraph 4. _____

Paragraph 5. _____

Paragraph 6. _____

Paragraph 7. _____

Paragraph 8. _____

Paragraph 9. _____

Paragraph 10. _____

26.2 The Author thinks

One of the hardest questions to answer in a comprehension is what the author thinks about a topic. The question is really asking what the narrator thinks. It uses higher order thinking skills and requires you to look at both the content and the language the author uses.

Some questions to help determine the view of the author include:

- What statements in the article show bias? What does that bias suggest?

- What opinions or belief statements are evident in the article?

- What evidence did the author include to support their opinions?

- What facts were missing?

- What words and phrases did the author use to present the information?

- Why did the author write this selection? Identifying the author's purpose helps to determine possible viewpoints, especially in persuasive writing.

Here are two short passages about dogs.

| Passage 1 | Dogs have been known as man's best friend. Besides being cute and providing companionship some people even owe their very lives to these creatures. |
| Passage 2 | Dogs earn some people a lot of money in racing. Originating from wolves, dogs are responsible for an average of two deaths a year in the UK. |

Is there a difference in how the author views dogs between the two passages?

Generally it is necessary to read the whole passage and understand the overall meaning in order to answer the question on what the author thinks, as a small section may be misleading.

Exercise 26.2

Read the following passages and answer the questions.

An excerpt from "The Poor Child's Toy" by Charles Baudelaire

On a highway, behind the gate of a vast garden, at the end of which could be discerned the white hues of a pretty manor house bathed in sunlight, was a beautiful, fresh child, clad in those country clothes that are so coquettish. Luxury, freedom from cares, the habitual sight of riches make such children so pretty that one is tempted to consider them moulded of a different substance from the children of mediocrity and poverty.

Beside him, lying on the grass, was a splendid toy, as fresh as its owner, varnished, gilded, clad in a crimson cloak and covered with plumes and glass beads. But the child was taking no notice of his favourite toy, and this is what he was looking at:

On the other side of the gate, out on the roadway, among the nettles and thistles, was another child, dirty, sickly, soiled with soot, one of those pariah-kids in whom an impartial eye would discover beauty, as the eye of a connoisseur can divine an ideal painting underneath a layer of tarnish, if only the repugnant patina of poverty were washed away.

1. What does the author think about poverty?

_____

_____

2. How do you know?

_____

_____

3. What do you think the word "patina" means in the last line?

_____

4. Why does the author mention the physical appearance of the poor child in the last paragraph?

_____

_____

Read the following short paragraphs and answer the questions that follow.

5. For Valentine's Day, my thoughtful neighbour gave his wife a poem that took him about two seconds to write. Gosh.

What does the author think of his neighbour?

_____

6. Anna lives just up the road from me. I went to school with her and have known her all my life, but if she died, I wouldn't go to her funeral.

What does the author think of Anna?

_____

7. No, there is no need to spend a lot of money on my birthday present. Just having you for a husband is better than any gift money could buy. In fact, I'll just drive my old rusty bucket of bolts into town and buy myself something small. And if the poor old car doesn't break down, I'll be back soon.

What is the main point of the passage?

_____

_____

"You are what you eat," is a common saying, as what a person eats can have a profound effect on their health, looks, how they feel and their level of energy. There is plenty of fresh fruit and vegetables, whole grain products and lean meat for a nutritious diet. However, the plethora of convenience foods and processed ingredients; as well as soft-drinks, cakes, biscuits, chocolates and sweets prove to be too enticing for many. Full of: sugars, hydrogenated fats, colourings and preservatives, all of which can be harmful if eaten in excess, the consequences of poor health, obesity and a lack of energy are becoming a reality for many. The situation is becoming critical and it has been said that the children of today may be the first generation who die younger than their parents.

8. What is the main point of the passage?

   _____

9. What is the purpose of the word harmful in the passage?

   _____

10. A railway station of a cold winter's night is a depressing place. Cold, wet, frozen people mill, eyes peeled for the sight of their train. Their breath, dragon-like, wind howling like an angry beast, they were drawing their jumpers and coats tighter around them when the announcement came over the speakers: "All trains have been cancelled. Sorry for the inconvenience and we wish you a good night."

   What is the main point of the first four lines of the passage?

   _____

26.3 The Meaning of Words

One common type of comprehension question is to provide the meaning of a word in the passage, or choose a synonym that could be used to replace the word.

In this type of question it is essential that the word is read in the context of the passage.

Example: The eagle scanned the horizon with his keen eyesight, alert for any sign of prey.

What word can be used to replace the word keen in the above sentence?

a. Enthusiastic
b. Good
c. Shrewd
d. Interest

While keen generally means enthusiastic, that does not fit in the context of the sentence. The answer is (b) good, making the sentence "The eagle scanned the horizon with his good eyesight."

If a word is used that you do not know, then treat the question like a cloze and look at which word would make sense.

Example: The professor was very respected by the students. His sagacity was helpful to them as they developed a rich understanding in the field. The professor was known to use his experience, insight, and common sense to help his students pursue their dreams.

What does the word sangacity mean?

      a. Wisdom.

      b. Thoughtlessness.

      c. Carelessness.

      d. Mannerisms.

From the context, it is clear that wisdom would make sense. When I insert wisdom into the sentence it reads: His wisdom was helpful to them as they developed a rich understanding in the field; which makes sense.

So, wisdom is the answer.

Exercise 26.3

Read this passage from "The Velveteen Rabbit" by Margery Williams, and answer the questions below:

1   There was once a velveteen rabbit, and in the beginning he was really splendid.

2   He was fat and bunchy, as a rabbit should be; his coat was spotted brown and

3   white, he had real thread whiskers, and his ears were lined with pink sateen.

4   On Christmas morning, when he sat wedged in the top of the Boy's stocking,

5   with a sprig of holly between his paws, the effect was charming.

6

7   There were other things in the stocking, nuts and oranges and a toy engine,

8   and chocolate almonds and a clockwork mouse, but the Rabbit was quite the

9   best of all. For at least two hours the Boy loved him, and then Aunts and

10   Uncles came to dinner, and there was a great rustling of tissue paper and

11   unwrapping of parcels, and in the excitement of looking at all the new presents

12   the Velveteen Rabbit was forgotten.

13

14   For a long time he lived in the toy cupboard or on the nursery floor, and no one

15   thought very much about him. He was naturally shy, and being only made of

16   velveteen, some of the more expensive toys quite snubbed him. The

17   mechanical toys were very superior, and looked down upon every one else;

18   they were full of modern ideas, and pretended they were real. The model boat,

19   who had lived through two seasons and lost most of his paint, caught the tone

20   from them and never missed an opportunity of referring to his rigging in

21   technical terms. The Rabbit could not claim to be a model of anything, for he

22   didn't know that real rabbits existed; he thought they were all stuffed with

23   sawdust like himself, and he understood that sawdust was quite out-of-date

24 and should never be mentioned in modern circles. Even Timothy, the jointed

25 wooden lion, who was made by the disabled soldiers, and should have had

26 broader views, put on airs and pretended he was connected with Government.

27 Between them all the poor little Rabbit was made to feel himself very

28 insignificant and commonplace, and the only person who was kind to him at all

29 was the Skin Horse.

1. What word could be used to replace the word "wedged" in line 4?

    a. Tapered.

    b. Chock.

    c. Squeezed.

    d. Blocked.

2. What word could be used to replace the word "charming" in line 5?

    a. Handsome.

    b. Delightful.

    c. Affectionate.

    d. Annoying.

3. What word could be used to replace the word "clockwork" in line 8?

    a. Wind-up.

    b. Accurate.

    c. Regular.

    d. Timely.

4. What word could be used to replace the word "naturally" in line 15?

    a. Normally

    b. Living.

    c. Earth.

    d. Exterior.

5. What word could be used to replace the word "snubbed" in line 16?

    a. Insult.

    b. Moved.

    c. Rubbed.

    d. Ignored.

6. What word could be used to replace the word "superior" in line 17?

    a. Better.

    b. Surpassing.

    c. Pompous.

    d. Chief.

7. What word could be used to replace the word "seasons" in line 19?

   a. Time periods.

   b. Condiments.

   c. Flavourings.

   d. Acclimatisations.

8. What word could be used to replace the words "referring to" in line 20?

   a. Dealing with.

   b. In relation to.

   c. In respect to.

   d. Talking about.

9. What word could be used to replace the words "out-of-date" in line 23?

   a. Current.

   b. Currant.

   c. Old-fashioned.

   d. Useless

10. What word could be used to replace the word "views" in line 26?

   a. Vision.

   b. Perspective.

   c. Scenery.

   d. Impression.

Chapter 27: Comprehension – Three Types of Question

27.1 Textual Questions

Reading comprehension refers to the understanding and analysis of written English passages. While the simplest questions involve a simple understanding of the words and finding the answer in the passage; more difficult questions require analysis and interpretation.

There are three types of questions in comprehension passages:

- Textual - The answer can be located in the text.
- Context - Requires an understanding of the surrounding text.
- Evaluative - Requires an understanding of what the passage is about as a whole and put together different aspects of the text.

In the simplest of these question types, the answer can simply be found in the text.

Example: John drove his red car over the green hill and through the valley, alongside the meandering river.

What colour is John's car?

Answer: Red.

Read the passage below. Then answer the questions giving both the answer and the line number where the answer is found.

The Adventures of Pinocchio
by C. Collodi (Pseudonym of Carlo Lorenzini)
Translated from the Italian by Carol Della Chiesa

1 As soon as he reached home, Geppetto took his tools and began to cut and
2 shape the wood into a Marionette.

3 "What shall I call him?" he said to himself. "I think I'll call him Pinocchio. This
4 name will make his fortune. I knew a whole family of Pinocchi once--Pinocchio
5 the father, Pinocchia the mother, and Pinocchi the children--and they were all
6 lucky. The richest of them begged for his living."

7 After choosing the name for his Marionette, Geppetto set seriously to work to
8 make the hair, the forehead, the eyes. Fancy his surprise when he noticed that
9 these eyes moved and then stared fixedly at him. Geppetto, seeing this, felt
10 insulted and said in a grieved tone:

11 "Ugly wooden eyes, why do you stare so?"

12 There was no answer.

13 After the eyes, Geppetto made the nose, which began to stretch as soon as
14 finished. It stretched and stretched and stretched till it became so long, it
15 seemed endless.

16 Poor Geppetto kept cutting it and cutting it, but the more he cut, the longer
17 grew that impertinent nose. In despair he let it alone.

18 Next he made the mouth.

19 No sooner was it finished than it began to laugh and poke fun at him.

20 "Stop laughing!" said Geppetto angrily; but he might as well have spoken to
21 the wall.

22 "Stop laughing, I say!" he roared in a voice of thunder.

23 The mouth stopped laughing, but it stuck out a long tongue.

24 Not wishing to start an argument, Geppetto made believe he saw nothing and
25 went on with his work. After the mouth, he made the chin, then the neck, the
26 shoulders, the stomach, the arms, and the hands.

27 As he was about to put the last touches on the finger tips, Geppetto felt his wig
28 being pulled off. He glanced up and what did he see? His yellow wig was in the
29 Marionette's hand. "Pinocchio, give me my wig!"

30 But instead of giving it back, Pinocchio put it on his own head, which was half
31 swallowed up in it.

32 At that unexpected trick, Geppetto became very sad and downcast, more so
33 than he had ever been before.

34 "Pinocchio, you wicked boy!" he cried out. "You are not yet finished, and you
35 start out by being impudent to your poor old father. Very bad, my son, very
36 bad!"

37 And he wiped away a tear.

38 The legs and feet still had to be made. As soon as they were done, Geppetto
39 felt a sharp kick on the tip of his nose.

40 "I deserve it!" he said to himself. "I should have thought of this before I made
41 him. Now it's too late!"

42 He took hold of the Marionette under the arms and put him on the floor to
43 teach him to walk.

44 Pinocchio's legs were so stiff that he could not move them, and Geppetto held
45 his hand and showed him how to put out one foot after the other.

46 When his legs were limbered up, Pinocchio started walking by himself and ran
47 all around the room. He came to the open door, and with one leap he was out
48 into the street. Away he flew!

1. What colour was Geppetto's wig?

    _____ line answer on: _____

2. What was the first surprise Geppetto had in the passage?

    _____ line answer on: _____

3. How did Geppetto feel when the eyes stared at him?

    _____ line answer on: _____

4. What did Pinocchio do when he stopped laughing?

    _____ line answer on: _____

5. What was the first thing Pinocchio did with his hands?

    _____ line answer on: _____

6. What did Geppetto teach Pinocchio to do in the passage?

    _____ line answer on: _____

7. What did Pinocchio kick when he had legs?

    _____ line answer on: _____

8. How did it make Gepetto feel when Pinnocchio laughed and made fun of him?

    _____ line answer on: _____

9. How did Geppetto view himself in relation to Pinocchio?

    _____ line answer on: _____

10. Why did Pinocchio find it hard to move his legs at first?

    _____ line answer on: _____

27.2 Context and Evaluative Questions

When looking at a text it can help to ask "the five W's":

- Who
- What
- When
- Where
- Why

Contextual questions require an understanding of the passage immediately before and after the relevant portion of the text. Answering the question is not as obvious as with factual questions.

Evaluative questions require gaining an understanding of the entire passage. It may require you to work out the main idea, compare and contrast different parts of the text, determine the importance of the different sections, decide whether or not there is any bias, work out what the view of the author is and work out any moral to the passage. These are the most difficult questions to answer.

Example: Read the excerpt below from "The World I Live in" by Helen Keller.

My hand is to me what your hearing and sight together are to you. In large measure we travel the same highways, read the same books, speak the same language, yet our experiences are different. All my comings and goings turn on the hand as on a pivot. It is the hand that binds me to the world of men and women. The hand is my feeler with which I reach through isolation and darkness and seize every pleasure, every activity that my fingers encounter. With the dropping of a little word from another's hand into mine, a slight flutter of the fingers, began the intelligence, the joy, the fullness of my life.

1. With what part of her body does Helen Keller access the world?
   a. Eyes.
   b. Ears.
   c. Hands.
   d. Feet.

2. In this passage what does Helen Keller mean when she writes that we travel on the same highways?
   a. She drives on the same streets and roads as her readers.
   b. Her experiences are the same as ours.
   c. We share the same way of life.
   d. We wear the same shoes.

3. What type of writing is this?
   a. Novel.
   b. Biography.
   c. Encyclopaedia entry.
   d. Textbook.

In the first question, we are asked what part of the body Helen Keller uses to access the world. The passage clearly informs the reader that Helen Keller accesses the world through the hand; particularly in the first sentence when the passage states that "My hand is to me what your hearing and sight together are to you." So the first answer is her hands.

In question 2 of the example, we are asked what it means that "we travel on the same highways." This is asking you to recognise metaphorical (figurative) language. As this phrase is not literal, it cannot be answers A or D. Her experience is different to us, as in the second sentence it says "yet our experiences are different". However, the passage says that the world we live is the same and she is accessing the same world with her hands. So the answer to the second question is that "We share the same way of life."

In question 3 of the example, we are asked for the type of writing. As it is about some-one (Helen Keller) it is a biography (We can refer to it more specifically as an autobiography as the author, Helen Keller, is talking about herself. An autobiography is a type of biography).

So the answers will look like this:

1. With what part of her body does Helen Keller access the world?
   a. Eyes
   b. Ears
   c. <u>Hands</u>
   d. Feet

2. In this passage what does Helen Keller mean when she writes that we travel on the same highways?
   a. She drives on the same streets and roads as her readers
   b. Her experiences are the same as ours
   c. <u>We share the same way of life</u>
   d. We wear the same shoes

3. What type of writing is this?
   a. Novel
   b. <u>Biography</u>
   c. Encyclopaedia entry
   d. Textbook

Read the following:

Tigers are the largest of the cat family. Tigers have been described as conservation dependent. Of the eight species of tiger, three have already become extinct in the last sixty years. All of the remaining species of tiger are endangered. Three are critically endangered. In the wild there are now only about 4000 tigers compared to 100 000 in the early 1900s.

The Sumatran tiger is the smallest of the tiger species and lives exclusively on the island of Sumatra in Indonesia. There are now fewer than 500 Sumatran tigers remaining, of which 270 are in captive breeding programmes.

Reasons that the Sumatran tiger has become endangered include poaching for tiger skins, alternative Asian medicines made from tiger bone and other parts of the tiger, habitat loss, weather and other natural disasters.

While people have caused the demise of the Sumatran tiger, people are also helping the tiger to survive. Zoos around the world are participating in a captive breeding programme. Much of the tigers' existing habitat is now protected. International agreements make it illegal to buy, sell or import tiger products. Hopefully the education programmes, tiger reserves and captive breeding programme will enable this iconic species to survive into the next century.

1. What does the author mean by "conservation dependent"?
    a. The tiger is a great advertisement for conservation.
    b. The tiger is increasing in number due to conservation.
    c. The tiger will only survive due to the efforts of conservation programmes.
    d. Conservation programmes rely on the tiger.

2. According to the passage, which of the following is true?
   a. The Sumatran tiger is the most endangered of the remaining tigers.
   b. The Sumatran tiger only lives in Sumatra, an island of Indonesia.
   c. The tiger is no longer used in alternative medicines.
   d. Sumatran tigers are small.

3. Which word best describes the author's view of the position of the Sumatran tiger in the world today.
   a. Precarious.
   b. Universal.
   c. Carnivorous.
   d. Improving rapidly.

4. How does the author see the role of people with regards to the Sumatran tiger?
   a. Negative – the main reason for the tiger's decline.
   b. Positive – the way the tiger will survive into the future.
   c. Both the reason for the decline and the way that the tiger can survive into the future.
   d. Neutral.

5. What book might you find the above passage in?
   a. A novel.
   b. A handbook.
   c. A zoo newsletter.
   d. An atlas.

Read the following passage from The Brothers Fairy Tales, "The Fox and the Cat."

It happened that the cat met the fox in a forest, and as she thought to herself: "He is clever and full of experience, and much esteemed in the world," she spoke to him in a friendly way. "Good day, dear Mr. Fox, how are you? How is all with you? How are you getting on in these hard times?" The fox, full of all kinds of arrogance, looked at the cat from head to foot, and for a long time did not know whether he would give any answer or not. At last he said: "Oh, you wretched beard-cleaner, you piebald fool, you hungry mouse-hunter, what can you be thinking of? Have you the cheek to ask how I am getting on? What have you learnt? How many arts do you understand?" "I understand but one," replied the cat, modestly. "What art is that?" asked the fox. "When the hounds are following me, I can spring into a tree and save myself." "Is that all?" said the fox. "I am master of a hundred arts, and have into the bargain a sackful of cunning. You make me sorry for you; come with me, I will teach you how people get away from the hounds." Just then came a hunter with four dogs. The cat sprang nimbly up a tree, and sat down at the top of it, where the branches and foliage quite concealed her. "Open your sack, Mr. Fox, open your sack," cried the cat to him, but the dogs had already seized him, and were holding him fast. "Ah, Mr. Fox," cried the cat. "You with your hundred arts are left in the lurch! Had you been able to climb like me, you would not have lost your life."

6. When the cat first meets the fox, the cat thinks that the fox is?
    a. Deceitful and full of cunning.
    b. Clever and full of experience.
    c. Friendly and eager to talk.
    d. Shy and fearful.

7. Where does the cat meet the fox?
    a. Tree behind branches and foliage.
    b. Creek.
    c. Forest.
    d. Meadow.

8. What is meant by the word arrogance?
    a. Clever.
    b. Has lots of courage.
    c. Thinking oneself superior.
    d. Sly and deceitful.

9. Many morals have been suggested for this tale. Which of the following cannot be concluded from this story?
    a. It is better to have one good talent than many talents.
    b. Arrogance does not pay.
    c. Be friendly.
    d. A little common sense is better than many clever tricks.

10. What type of writing is this?
    a. Fairytale.
    b. Legend.
    c. Drama.
    d. Biography.

27.3 Comprehension of Prose

The comprehension of prose in the 11 Plus can contain textual, contextual, and evaluative questions. It can contain questions asking the meaning of individual words as well as what types of words they are.

Exercise 27.3

Read the passage on Fingerprinting, then answer the questions below.

Fingerprinting is used globally for personal identification. It is used by every police organisation in the world to place criminals at crime scenes and also by any industry that requires an accurate identification of personnel.

Remarkably, no two fingerprints have been found to be alike amongst the world's millions of people.

Fingerprints are developed in the uterus and their formation remains in place throughout life, in a series of 'whorls', 'arches' and 'accidentals'. Even if the skin on a person's fingers is injured in some way, when the wound heals the fingerprints return to their original pattern. Even if the scars on the fingers are permanent it is not unusual for there to be sufficient structure left for identification purposes.

Even identical twins have unique fingerprints, despite their matched DNA.

Who discovered fingerprinting?

The history of fingerprinting goes a long way back to the clever Qin Dynasty (around 220BC) in China when burglars were caught through fingerprint identification. This was probably the earliest evidence of forensic investigation.

Throughout history police forces everywhere have tried to keep tabs on the criminal fraternity by keeping records of personal appearance. Artists' impressions, photographs and even personal description by people known to have outstanding memory retention have all been tried and tested. The problem has always been that peoples' personal appearance will change from time to time and even personal measurements can alter with body weight and age.

In the 1870s, Alphonse Bertillon, a French anthropologist, developed the 'Bertillon System', a way of measuring and recording body parts. The system was relied upon for around 30 years until it was discovered that two prisoners in a Kansas prison were almost identical: fingerprinting cleared up the confusion in the end.

A professional forensic organisation was established in 1915: the International Association for Identification (IAI). And in 1977 the Certified Latent Print Examiner (CLPE) programme was given authority to issue certification for agencies to use fingerprints as a means of evidence. The CLPE could also review fingerprinting units and shut down any service they deemed to be incompetent.

Fingerprinting has been the basis of more convictions than any other form of forensic evidence, including DNA testing, first used in 1986 by Dr Alec J. Jeffreys of Leicester University.

How are fingerprints taken and used in evidence?

'Exemplar prints' is the name given to fingerprints collected with the subject's permission, to be used for enrolment in a college, job or even following an arrest.

A set of exemplar prints would usually feature one print from each finger and also the thumbs. The finger is rolled upon an inked pad or whatever material is being used for the impression, from the edge of one nail to the other. Alternatively modern prints might be collected by live scan before being forwarded electronically.

'Latent' prints are those left behind at a crime scene which may be captured and examined by investigators at a later time. Interestingly, even partial prints may be used to identify a person.

Crime scene investigators use powder that adheres to residue left by friction ridge skin on fingers, palms and also feet. The powder is gently applied to surfaces using an ultra-fine brush, revealing the prints which can then be processed and copied to databases for comparison with an archive. Fingerprinting is useful not only to identify criminals but also to eliminate innocent parties from a crime scene. The impression of a fingerprint can also be used as identification to gain access to computers, security systems, cars, cell phones...

The science of fingerprinting is called 'dactylography', from the Greek words 'daktylos' meaning 'finger' and 'skopein' meaning 'to examine' - whereas the study of skin friction ridges is called 'dermatoglyphics'.

1. Which industries use fingerprinting?
   a. The police.
   b. The armed forces.
   c. A range of industries.
   d. All of the above.

2. Which police agencies use fingerprinting?
   a. Local police forces.
   b. Scotland Yard.
   c. Special forensic police units.
   d. Police forces all over the world.

3. Who discovered fingerprinting?
   a. Sherlock Holmes.
   b. The Chinese in the Qin Dynasty.
   c. The Greeks.
   d. Dr Alec J. Jeffreys.

4. Why has personal appearance not always been successful in identifying criminals?
   a. Personal appearance can change.
   b. Photographs are too difficult to archive.
   c. Artists' impressions are not good enough.
   d. People's memories are unreliable.

5. Which professional forensic organisation was established in 1915?
    a. The Metropolitan Police.
    b. International Association for Identification.
    c. The Coroner's Office.
    d. Certified Latent Print Examiner.

6. Who was Alphonse Bertillon?
    a. A police detective.
    b. A French anthropologist.
    c. A pathologist.
    d. A forensic scientist.

7. How long was the 'Bertillon System' used to identify criminals?
    a. Around 30 years.
    b. A month.
    c. Two weeks in the 1870s.
    d. Sixty-two years.

8. How did the 'Bertillon System' work?
    a. It measured and recorded body parts thought to be unique.
    b. Through the use of photographs taken from archive.
    c. By the process of elimination.
    d. An early fingerprint system, using photographs of the tops of fingers.

9. Which fingerprinting authority was established in 1977?
    a. International Association for Identification.
    b. Certified Latent Print Examiner.
    c. Leicester University.
    d. Scotland Yard.

10. Where could this article be found?
    a. In a newspaper.
    b. In a manual.
    c. In a newsletter.
    d. In an encyclopaedia.

11. What other form of forensic identification was first used in 1986?
    a. Fingerprinting.
    b. DNA testing.
    c. Photo ID.
    d. Latent prints.

12. Where did Dr Alec J. Jeffreys work?
    a. In a prison.
    b. At a police station.
    c. At Leicester University.
    d. International Association for Identification.

13. What is used to capture latent fingerprints?
    a. Liquid.
    b. Powder.
    c. Glass jars.
    d. Inked pad.

14. Where are prints stored once they have been copied?
    a. In buff folders.
    b. On a computer.
    c. In police cells.
    d. In a filing cabinet
       .

15. Can fingerprints be used as identification to gain access to computers?
    a. Yes.
    b. No.
    c. Only in conjunction with photo ID.
    d. Not yet, but in the future they will be.

16. What is the science of fingerprinting called?
    a. Dactylography.
    b. Dermatology.
    c. Forensic science.
    d. Dactylology.

17. At what age do fingerprints develop?
    a. At puberty.
    b. Before birth.
    c. At around 18.
    d. As a young baby.

18. Do twins have identical fingerprints?
    a. Yes, always.
    b. No, never.
    c. Only if they are identical twins.
    d. Only if they are non-identical twins.

19. What is the subject of the science of dermatoglyphics?
    a. The science of fingerprinting.
    b. Skin types.
    c. Finger painting.
    d. The study of skin friction ridges.

20. What are 'latent' prints?
    a. Fingerprints that were left too late to be of any use.
    b. Prints left at a crime scene that could be examined later.
    c. Fingerprints from animals other than humans.
    d. Prints from body parts other than fingers such as palms and the feet.

Chapter 28: Comprehension – Poetic Devices

28.1 Comparisons

One of the reasons why students tend to find poetry harder than prose, is that poetry normally uses much more imagery.

Similes, metaphors and personification:

- A **simile** compares two things using the word 'as' or 'like.'
  Example: The stars sparkled like diamonds in the sky.
- A **metaphor** compares two things without using 'as' or 'like.'
  Example: The glittering diamonds winked brightly as I looked up at the night sky.
- **Personification** is giving a human characteristic to an animal, object or idea.
  Example: The stars danced in the moonlit sky.

Exercise 28.1
Read the poem "Sleep" by Annie Matheson and then answer the questions below:

Soft silence of the summer night!
Alive with wistful murmurings,
Enfold me in thy quiet might:
Shake o'er my head thy slumb'rous wings,
So cool and light:
Let me forget all earthly things
In sleep to-night!

Tired roses, passionately sweet,
Are leaning on their cool green leaves,
The mignonette[1] about my feet
A maze of tangled fragrance weaves,
Where dewdrops meet:
Kind sleep the weary world bereaves
Of noise and heat.

White lilies, pure as falling snow,
And redolent[2] of tenderness,
Are gently swaying to and fro,
Lulled by the breath of evening less
Than by the low
Music of sleepy winds, that bless
The buds that grow.

The air is like a mother's hand
Laid softly on a throbbing brow,
And o'er the darksome, dewy land
The peace of heaven is stealing now,
While, hand in hand,
Young angels tell the flowers how
Their lives are planned.

From yon deep sky the quiet stars
Look down with steadfast eloquence,
And God the prison-door unbars
That held the mute world's inmost sense
From all the wars
Of day's loud hurry and turbulence;
And nothing now the silence mars
Of love intense.

Notes:
1. A plant with spikes of small fragrant flowers
2. Strongly reminiscent or suggestive of something

Identify two examples of simile.

1. _____

2. _____

Identify two examples of metaphor.

3. _____

4. _____

Identify three examples of personification.

5. _____

6. _____

7. _____

What is the mood of the poem?

8. _____

"Twinkle, twinkle little star,

How I wonder what you are?

Up above the world so high,

Like a diamond in the sky."

9. Does the above poem use simile, metaphor or personification?

_____

All the world's a stage,

And all the men and women merely players;

They have their exits and their entrances,

And one man in his time plays many parts,

His acts being seven ages.

10. Does the above extract by William Shakespeare use simile, metaphor or personification?

_____

28.2 Poem sounds

Other literary techniques found in poetry include:

- **Rhyming** - two words rhyme when their last syllable sounds the same. They may or may not be spelled the same.
- **Rhythm** - a sense of beat.
- **Alliteration** - repetition of the consonant sound at the start of words, that are close together. They do not need to be spelled the same.
- **Assonance** - repetition of a vowel sound.
- **Consonance** - repetition of a consonant sound, particularly the consonant sound at the end of words.
- **Onomatopaeia** - a word that sounds like its meaning.
- **Hyperbole -** not a use of sound, but hyperbole or exaggeration is a technique frequently used in poetry for emphasis and to make a point.

All of these literary techniques help to make poems expressive and enhance their meaning.

Example:
Only in Sleep by Sara Teasdale

Only in sleep I see their faces,
Children I played with when I was a child,
Louise comes back with her brown hair braided,
Annie with ringlets warm and wild.

Only in sleep Time is forgotten —
What may have come to them, who can know?
Yet we played last night as long ago,
And the doll-house stood at the turn of the stair.

The years had not sharpened their smooth round faces,
I met their eyes and found them mild —
Do they, too, dream of me, I wonder,
And for them am I too a child?

The poem "Only in Sleep" by Sara Teasdale is written from the perspective of an old lady looking back on her life and remembering her childhood friends in her dreams.

Rhyme: 1st stanza – child, wild

2nd stanza – know, ago

3rd stanza – mild, child

Rhythm: no obvious rhythm

Alliteration (1st stanza): 3rd line – back, brown, braided

4th line – warm, wild

Assonance (3rd stanza): 2nd line – eyes, mild

3rd line – dream, me

Exercise 28.2

The Eagle
by Lord Alfred Tennyson

He clasps the crag with crooked hands;

Close to the sun in lonely lands,

Ringed with the azure world, he stands.

The wrinkled sea beneath him crawls;

He watches from his mountain walls,

And like a thunderbolt he falls.

1. What rhyming is in the poem?

    _____

    _____

2. Give an example of alliteration in the poem.

    _____

3. Give an example of hyperbole in the poem.

    _____

A Child's Garden

by Rudyard Kipling

Now there is nothing wrong with me

Except -- I think it's called T.B.

And that is why I have to lay

Out in the garden all the day.

Our garden is not very wide

And cars go by on either side,

And make an angry-hooty noise

That rather startles little boys.

But worst of all is when they take

Me out in cars that growl and shake,

With charabancs[1] so dreadful-near

I have to shut my eyes for fear.

128

But when I'm on my back again,

I watch the Croydon aeroplane

That flies across to France, and sings

Like hitting thick piano-strings.

When I am strong enough to do

The things I'm truly wishful to,

I'll never use a car or train

But always have an aeroplane;

And just go zooming round and round,

And frighten Nursey with the sound,

And see the angel-side of clouds,

And spit on all those motor-crowds!

Note:

1.   A charabanc was an early type of bus.

4. Describe the pattern of rhyming in the poem.

_____

_____

5. Give two examples of consonance in the fourth verse.

_____

_____

6. Give two examples of onomatopoeia from the second verse.

_____

_____

7. Give an example of onomatopoeia from the third verse.

_____

'Twas later when the summer went

by Emily Dickinson

'Twas later when the summer went

Than when the cricket came,

And yet we knew that gentle clock

Meant nought but going home.

'Twas sooner when the cricket went

Than when the winter came,

Yet that pathetic pendulum

Keeps esoteric time.

8. Give an example of alliteration in the poem.

   _____

9. Give an example of consonance in the poem.

   _____

10. Give an example of assonance in the poem.

   _____

Chapter 29: Comprehension – Poetic Imagery and Meaning

29.1 Imagery

The main thing that makes poetry comprehension so difficult is the use of imagery. So, the first task when doing comprehension of poetry is to work out what the imagery stands for. To do this, often the whole poem needs to be read through first.

Example:

The Coin

By Sara Teasdale

Into my heart's treasury

I slipped a coin

That time cannot take

Nor a thief purloin, —

Oh better than the minting

Of a gold-crowned king

Is the safe-kept memory

Of a lovely thing.

The above poem contains a lot of imagery. The coin represents a memory. While it is clear that it is an image from the beginning as you cannot put a real coin in your heart, that it is a memory is only clear after reading through the poem as a whole.

The heart is compared to a treasury or bank, where not money but memories are stored.

So the poem is saying that unlike money, memories cannot be stolen or diminished by time and that they are more valuable.

Exercise 29.1

Winter Time

By Robert Louis Stevenson

Late lies the wintry sun a-bed,

A frosty, fiery sleepy-head;

Blinks but an hour or two; and then,

A blood-red orange, sets again.

Before the stars have left the skies,

At morning in the dark I rise;

And shivering in my nakedness,

By the cold candle, bathe and dress.

Close by the jolly fire I sit

To warm my frozen bones a bit;

Or with a reindeer-sled, explore

The colder countries round the door.

When to go out, my nurse[1] doth wrap

Me in my comforter and cap;

The cold wind burns my face, and blows

Its frosty pepper up my nose.

Black are my steps on silver sod[2];

Thick blows my frosty breath abroad;

And tree and house, and hill and lake,

Are frosted like a wedding-cake.

Note:

1. A woman who has the general care of a child or children.
2. The surface of the ground, with the grass growing on it.

1. What does the blood red orange in the first verse refer to?

   _____

2. Give two examples of personification in the first verse.

   _____

   _____

3. What is Robert Louis Stevenson saying with this personification?

   _____

4. Give an example of alliteration in the second verse?

   _____

5. What affect does the alliteration have on the poem?

   _____

   _____

6. Is the candle really cold? Why does Robert Louis Stevenson describe the candle as cold?

   _____

   _____

7. What do the last two lines of the poem mean?

   _____

   _____

The Rainbow

By Christina Rossetti

Boats sail on the rivers,

And ships sail on the seas;

But clouds that sail across the sky

Are prettier than these.

There are bridges on the rivers,

As pretty as you please;

But the bow that bridges heaven,

And overtops the trees,

And builds a road from earth to sky,

Is prettier far than these.

8. The word sail is repeated in the first three lines. What effect does this have?

_____

_____

9. What is the bow that is referred to in the third line of the second verse?

_____

10. What is the meaning of the poem?

_____

_____

29.2 The Meaning of Poetry

As with prose, the first task in doing a comprehension on a piece of poetry is to determine what the main meaning of the poem is.

Example:

Ozymandias

By Percy Bysshe Shelley

I met a traveller from an antique land

Who said: Two vast and trunkless legs of stone

Stand in the desert. Near them on the sand,

Half sunk, a shatter'd visage lies, whose frown

And wrinkled lip and sneer of cold command

Tell that its sculptor well those passions read

Which yet survive, stamp'd on these lifeless things,

The hand that mock'd them and the heart that fed.

And on the pedestal these words appear:

"My name is Ozymandias, king of kings:

Look on my works, ye Mighty, and despair!"

Nothing beside remains: round the decay

Of that colossal wreck, boundless and bare,

The lone and level sands stretch far away.

The meaning of the poem is not immediately clear. The subject of the poem is the ruins of a large statue of Ozymandias. Ozymandias is better known as Ramses II who was king of Egypt from 1279 BC for 66 years. He is often regarded as the greatest, and most powerful Pharaoh of the Egyptian Empire. The people referred to him as "King of Kings" because he was so powerful.

Now that the subject is understood,the meaning of the poem becomes clear. The ruins: "trunkless legs of stone," "a shattered visage (face)" are compared to the inscription of how great Ozymandias was. This leads the reader to the understanding that if even Ozymandias' reign is reduced to nothing but broken stones in the desert then no matter how great a leader (or indeed we) may be, eventually they (or we) will die and nothing but ruins remain.

A number of interpretations have been suggested. One possible conclusion would be that no matter how successful you may become, you will still die and time will lessen your memory. So do not be too proud or arrogant.

Exercise 29.2

Read the poem below and answer the questions that follow.

The Fog
By W.H. Davies

I saw the fog grow thick
Which soon made blind my ken[1];
It made tall men of boys,
And giants of tall men.

It clutched my throat, I coughed;
Nothing was in my head
Except two heavy eyes
Like balls of burning lead.

And when it grew so black
That I could know no place
I lost all judgment then,
Of distance or of space.

The street lamps, and the lights
Upon the halted cars,
Could either be on earth
Or be the heavenly stars.

A man passed by me close,
I asked my way, he said,
"Come, follow me, my friend " -
I followed where he led.

He rapped the stones in front,
"Trust me," he said, " and come";
I followed like a child -
A blind man led me home.

Note:

1. Ken means one's knowledge or understanding.

1. What does the word blind mean in line 2?
    a. Unable to see.
    b. Lacking the ability to think clearly.
    c. Visually impaired.
    d. Insensitive.

2. What does the word blind mean in the last line?
    a. Unable to see.
    b. Lacking the ability to think clearly.
    c. Visually impaired.
    d. Insensitive.

3. What does "It made tall men of boys, and giants of tall men." suggest to the reader?
    a. The fog had changed how things looked.
    b. The fog meant that boys and men behaved differently.
    c. It made boys mature.
    d. It effected boys differently to girls.

4. What suggests that the fog was more than a thick mist of water droplets, but contained some kind of pollution?
    a. Which soon made blind my ken.
    b. It made tall men of boys.
    c. It clutched my throat, I coughed.
    d. And when it grew so black.

5. It clutched my throat and coughed means:
    a. The narrator was having trouble breathing because of the fog.
    b. The narrator had a sore throat.
    c. The fog and the narrator were fighting.
    d. The fog held the narrator by the throat and coughed.

6. The word halted shows that the cars were:
    a. Mobile.
    b. Stolen.
    c. Stationary.
    d. Damaged.

7. What do "The stones in front" in the last stanza refer to?
    a. Stones the blind man had in his pocket.
    b. Stones by the side of the road.
    c. The stones at the front of his house.
    d. The path they were on.

8. What was like balls of burning lead?
    a. Rocks on the road.
    b. Hailstones in the storm.
    c. The narrator's eyes.
    d. The feeling of the fog on the narrator's skin.

9. What does the last verse tell the reader?
    a. The blind man was lost too.
    b. The poet trusted the blind man.
    c. The fog won the battle that night.
    d. The poet could not return home.

10. Which statement could not be a meaning of the poem?
    a. People only trust what they can literally see and lack awareness of things unseen.
    b. As time passes even difficulties will pass. They don't stay permanently.
    c. Losing your sense of sight is very unsettling.
    d. Fog can cause breathing difficulties.

Workbooks

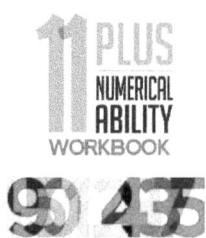 

Do you have the matching test books, created to be used alongside the workbooks.

  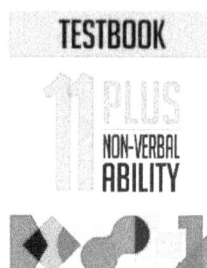

Vocabulary is an important part of your 11 Plus Preparation.

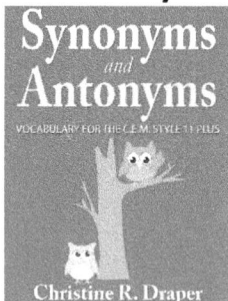

Lightning Source UK Ltd.
Milton Keynes UK
UKHW051003130921
390494UK00006B/228

9 781909 986114